Grammar Workshop

Level Blue

Beverly Ann Chin

Senior Series Consultant
Professor of English
University of Montana
Missoula, MT

Series Consultants

Elaine M. Czarnecki
Literacy Consultant
Annapolis, MD

Kerry A. Vann
Director of Language Arts
Hauppauge School District
Hauppauge, NY

Sadlier-Oxford
A Division of William H. Sadlier, Inc.

Reviewers

The publisher wishes to thank the following teachers for their thorough review and thoughtful comments on portions of the series prior to publication.

Jurodell Banks
Houston, TX

Patricia Cobb
Altamonte Springs, FL

Dr. George Grunfeld
Fort Lauderdale, FL

Margaret Hanna
Quincy, MA

Linda Sumner
Glenside, PA

Donna Wittouck
San Diego, CA

Photo Credits

Alamy/Big Cheese Photo LLC: 117; Corbis Premium Collection: 28; Paul Glendell: 25; John Henshall: 34; Andre Jenny: 168; coin Alan King: 177; Stan Kujawa: 118; David Lyons: 128; M. Timothy O'Keefe: 170; Gabe Palmer: 136; Purestock: 14; Frances Roberts: 228; Royalty Free: 172; Stock Connection Distribution: 139; Vision of America, LLC: 206; Wherett.com: 106. Andevan Bronzeworks, Inc., www.Andevan.com: 33. AP Photo/Jean-Marc Bouju: 82; stf: 148. Arkansas Parks & Tourism: 50. Art Resource, NY/Adoc-photos: 130; Terra Foundation for American Art, Chicago, Mary Cassatt (1844-1926), Summertime, c. 1894. Oil on canvas, 39 5/8 X 32 in. Daniel J. Terra Collection, 1988.25: 150. The Bridgeman Art Library/Feathered Coyote, c. 1500 (stone), Aztec, (16th century)/Museo Nacional de Anthropologia, Mexico City, Mexico: Photo: Michel Zabe/AZA: 19. Corbis/Yann Arthus-Bertrand: 203; Todd Gipstein: 220, 222. Getty Images/Blend Images/PBNJ Productions: 221; Blend Images/Ariel Skelley: 60; Hulton Archive/Three Lions: 152; Iconica/White Packert: 192; National Geographic/Stephen Alvarez: 156; Photodisc: 30; Photonica/Henrik Sorensen: 158; Riser/Kevin Schafer: 132; Stone/Daryl Benson: 200; Stone/Art Wolfe: 80; Taxi/Hitoshi Nishimura: 24; Taxi/Jagdeep Rajput: 133. The Image Works/Bob Daemmrich: 36. Masterfile/Peter Griffith: 48. Tony Mazzariello: 108. National Park Service Ellis Island Immigration Museum, www.ellisisland.com: 207. NASA: 169. iStockphoto/JPStrickler: 26. Photodisc: 8, 21, 93. Punchstock/Blend Images: 20; Digital Vision: 53, 90, 183, 202; Photodisc: 178, 224. Shutterstock/John Blanton: 157; Tyler Boyes: 214; Evan Dube: 142; Elena Elisseeva: 72; Sebastien Gauthier: 16; Hannah Geighorn: 12; Adam Gryko: 126; Inger Anne-Hulbaekdal: 76; Curtis Kautzer: 92; Cathy Keifer: 104; George Lee: 116; Maigi: 100; Glenda M. Powers: 56; Nathan Shahan: 140; Specta: 212; Christophe Testi: 204; VisualField: 88; Marek Walica: 124; Jerome Whittingham: 105. Milind Tulankar, www.jalatarang.com: 125. The U.S. National Archives & Records Administration: 110. V & A Images/Victoria & Albert Museum: 64.

Illustrators

Ron Berg: 29, 40, 42, 95, 102, 144, 146; Ken Bowser: 57, 77, 78, 112, 113, 114, 193, 194, 216, 217, 218; John Ceballos: 61, 62, 141, 180, 182, 208, 210; Mena Dolobowsky: 15, 65, 66, 138; CD Hullinger: 17, 84, 85, 86, 160, 161, 163, 188, 189, 190; Martin Lemelman: 10, 11, 154, 155; Zina Saunders: 23, 52, 54, 134, 174, 184, 186, 187, 225, 230, 231; Paul Weiner: 37, 38, 73, 75, 96, 97, 98

CONTENTS

ONLINE COMPONENTS
www.grammarworkshop.com

ONLINE COMPONENTS
www.grammarworkshop.com

ONLINE COMPONENTS
www.grammarworkshop.com

NOTE TO STUDENTS

You already know how to read, speak, and write English. So why should you learn grammar?

What Is Grammar?

Like all languages, English has rules about how words can be put together in sentences. Learning these rules will help you to speak and write so that everyone understands you. When you study grammar, you learn that words in English can be grouped into different parts. These parts include nouns, verbs, adjectives, adverbs, prepositions, and pronouns. Grammar tells you how to put these parts together correctly.

How Will Grammar Help You?

Knowing grammar will help you to become a better reader, speaker, and writer. Knowing how language works will help you to read with more understanding. It will help you to express your feelings and ideas clearly. Your writing will be easier to follow. You will also make fewer mistakes when you do homework and take tests.

What Is GRAMMAR WORKSHOP?

GRAMMAR WORKSHOP is designed to teach you the rules of English and to give you lots and lots of practice. This book is called a WORKSHOP because it teaches in ways that make you work. You don't just read and memorize. You have to Learn, Practice, and Write.

What's Inside GRAMMAR WORKSHOP, Level Blue?

GRAMMAR WORKSHOP, Level Blue, covers everything that students in your grade are expected to know. The book contains six units: **1** Sentences; **2** Nouns; **3** Verbs; **4** Adjectives, Adverbs, and Prepositions; **5** Pronouns; and **6** Capitalization and Punctuation. At the end of every unit, there are a two-page review and a two-page test.

What's in a Lesson?

LEARN Each four-page lesson begins with a Learn box that gives rules, definitions, and examples. In these lessons, the examples and exercises focus on a single theme. They present a great deal of information about animal migration, Vikings, instruments, and dozens of other interesting topics.

PRACTICE Three sets of practice exercises follow the Learn box. The first set is the easiest. It might ask you to identify or underline a grammatical element. The second set is a little harder, and the third is the most challenging. The third set usually asks you to correct mistakes in grammar in a piece of student writing.

WRITE The last page in the lesson may ask you to write original sentences, stories, or descriptions. Sometimes the writing task is to combine or revise sentences to make them more interesting.

Ready, Set, Go Grammar!

Remember how important it is to be able to speak and write well whenever you need to. It's time to get started. Have fun, learn those rules—and go grammar!

Lesson 1: **Kinds of Sentences**

LEARN

A **sentence** is a group of words that expresses a complete thought.

There are four kinds of sentences. Every sentence begins with a capital letter and ends with a punctuation mark. The end punctuation you use depends on the kind of sentence you write.

- A **declarative sentence** makes a statement. It ends with a period (.).

   The Moon is Earth's nearest neighbor.

- An **interrogative sentence** asks a question. It ends with a question mark (?).

   How far away is the Moon?

- An **imperative sentence** gives a command or makes a request. It ends with a period (.).

   Show me your photos of the Moon.

- An **exclamatory sentence** shows strong feelings. It ends with an exclamation mark (!).

   Wow, the full moon is so beautiful!
   What an amazing sight it is!

PRACTICE

A *Read each sentence. Write **declarative**, **interrogative**, **imperative**, or **exclamatory** to tell what kind of sentence it is.*

1. The Moon is about 385,000 kilometers away. _____

2. How many miles is that? _____

3. At 70 mph, you could drive to the Moon in 143 days. _____

4. Find out how fast a spaceship travels. _____

5. Astronauts have rocketed to the Moon in three days. _____

6. What an extraordinary trip that must be! _____

7. Tell me about conditions on the Moon. _____

8. Is the Moon really a dry, lifeless world? _____

9. At night, the temperature falls to –155° Celsius. _____

10. Brrrr, I can't even imagine such freezing cold! _____

B Add the correct punctuation mark at the end of each sentence. Then write *declarative, interrogative, imperative,* or *exclamatory* to tell what kind of sentence it is.

1. Can you guess how big the Moon is ____ _____

2. The Moon has five times the surface area of Australia ____ _____

3. Wow, that really surprises me ____ _____

4. Please tell me more about the Moon ____ _____

5. Why does the Moon seem to change its shape ____ _____

6. The Moon has no light of its own ____ _____

7. It only reflects sunlight ____ _____

8. Does Earth's gravity keep the Moon in orbit ____ _____

9. Look at these photos of the astronauts ____ _____

10. Hey, moonwalking looks like great fun ____ _____

Georgia has written a science fiction play about a trip to the Moon. The sentences in this scene have three missing capital letters and seven missing or incorrect end punctuation marks. Look for the mistakes, and correct them. Use the proofreading marks in the box.

Proofreading Marks

∧	Add
⊙	Period
ℓ	Take out
≡	Capital letter
/	Small letter

Captain Diaz please attach your oxygen lines.

Ben How long before we touch down.

(*The Excelsior craft bumps down on the rough surface.*)

Lisa There's your answer?

Ben Wow, what a thrill

Captain Diaz Prepare to open exit door *A*.

Ben Is there time for a photograph

Major Evans the mobile ranger unit is ready for boarding.

Lisa How far away is the moon settlement.

Ben our mapping system says 40 kilometers.

(*Ben suddenly trips over his oxygen line.*) Help,

I can't breathe.

Lisa (*reattaching the line*) Can you breathe okay now?

Ben (*nodding*): Whew, how clumsy I was

Captain Diaz Please prepare to enter the mobile unit.

Ben Watch me moonwalk.

Lisa (*climbing into mobile ranger*) Hooray,

this is one giant step for a woman!

Did you correct ten mistakes in capitalization and punctuation?

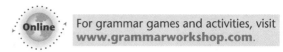
Online For grammar games and activities, visit
www.grammarworkshop.com.

WRITE

D *Imagine that you have just traveled to the first settlement on the Moon. Write one sentence that the person in each situation below might say. Write the kind of sentence that is given in parentheses. The first one is done for you.*

Situation 1 The leader of the settlement welcomes you to the Moon. The leader tells you what your job on the Moon will be. (declarative)

You will be a reporter on the *Daily Moon News*.

Situation 2 You don't understand something about your assignment. You ask the leader this question. (interrogative)

_____

_____

Situation 3 Another moon settler is surprised when he hears about the job you will do. He makes this statement to show his surprise. (exclamatory)

_____

_____

Situation 4 The leader gives you an assignment. The leader tells you to do it immediately. (imperative)

_____

_____

Situation 5 You and another moon settler are driving across the Moon in a moon vehicle. You express your amazement at the landscape. (exclamatory)

_____

_____

Proofreading Checklist ☑

❏ *Did you begin each sentence with a capital letter?*
❏ *Did you end each sentence with the correct end punctuation mark?*

Lesson 2: **Complete Subjects and Predicates**

LEARN

Every sentence has a subject and a predicate.

- The **complete subject** is made up of all the words that tell *whom* or *what* the sentence is about.

  A complete subject can be one word or more than one word.

    Several ancient civilizations developed in Mexico.
    Archaeologists study ancient civilizations.
    They learn about people's lives.

- The **complete predicate** is made up of all the words that tell what the subject *does* or *is*.

  A complete predicate can be one word or more than one word.

    Many advanced cultures **developed**.
    The Maya **are one example**.
    The Mayan civilization **began about 2300 years ago**.

Mayan calendar

PRACTICE

A *Read each sentence. Write **complete subject** or **complete predicate** to tell what part of the sentence is in **boldface**.*

1. Mayan farmers **grew large crops of corn**. _____

2. They fed a huge population. _____

3. Many people lived in Mayan cities. _____

4. Some **were artists, scientists, and historians**. _____

5. Stone palaces **lined some streets**. _____

6. The brightly painted buildings dazzled. _____

7. Temple carvings recorded dates and events. _____

8. The Maya **used two different calendars**. _____

9. These early people were good mathematicians. _____

10. Religion **was an important part of everyday life**. _____

B Draw a line between the complete subject and complete predicate of each sentence. Underline the complete subject once. Underline the complete predicate twice. The first one is done for you.

1. Archaeologists | learned a great deal about the Maya.

2. Most Maya worked in the fields.

3. Others completed building projects.

4. Skilled sculptors carved grand monuments.

5. These amazing sculptures thrill people today.

6. The Maya stopped work on holidays.

7. Many holidays were on the Mayan calendar.

8. Everyone gathered in the cities' plazas on these days.

9. Priests led special ceremonies.

10. Holiday celebrations included ball games.

11. Most Mayan cities had walled-in ball courts.

12. The Mayan ball game was a cross between basketball and soccer.

13. These games were played in honor of the Mayan gods.

14. Some cities had special buildings for astronomers.

15. Mayan astronomers studied the sun and stars.

C *Write a complete subject or a complete predicate to complete each sentence. Choose a subject or predicate from the box, or use a subject or predicate of your own. Write your sentence on the lines below, adding correct end punctuation.*

Remember
The **complete subject** tells *whom* or *what* the sentence is about.
The **complete predicate** tells what the subject *is* or *does*.

> stands for one day of the year   The Maya   This famous pyramid
> is an ancient Mayan temple   Many tourists

1. El Castillo _____

_____

2. visit the ancient pyramid today _____

_____

3. has 365 steps in all _____

_____

4. Each step _____

_____

5. deserted their cities after AD 900 _____

_____

El Castillo

WRITE

D On the lines below, write about a famous place that you have visited or would like to visit. Be creative. Make your visit sound so exciting that your friends will want to see the place, too. Be sure each sentence has a subject and a predicate.

_____

_____

_____

_____

_____

_____

_____

_____

_____

_____

Proofreading Checklist ✓

❑ *Does each sentence have a subject and a predicate?*
❑ *Does each sentence begin with a capital letter?*
❑ *Does each sentence have the correct end punctuation?*

Lesson 3: Simple Subjects and Predicates

LEARN

■ The **simple subject** is the most important word in the complete subject. It tells exactly *whom* or *what* the subject is about.

When the simple subject is one word or a name, the simple subject and the complete subject are the same. Most of the time, however, the simple subject is part of the complete subject.

■ The **simple predicate** is the most important word in the complete predicate. It tells exactly what the subject *does* or *is*.

The simple predicate may be one or more words. When it is one word, the simple predicate is the same as the complete predicate.

■ In the chart below, the simple subject and simple predicate are in **boldface**.

Complete Subject	Complete Predicate
The **man** at the computer	**writes**.
Dr. Lane	**has researched** a book about coyotes.
Coyotes	**inhabited** the Great Plains originally.
They	**hunt** alone or in pairs.

PRACTICE

A Write *simple subject, simple predicate, complete subject,* or *complete predicate* to tell what part of each sentence is in **boldface**.

1. An average coyote **weighs** about 30 pounds. _____

2. People **confuse** coyotes with dogs sometimes. _____

3. **A coyote's thick bushy tail** hangs low. _____

4. Most dogs **hold their tails high.** _____

5. Everyone **recognizes** the howl of a coyote. _____

6. The eerie **howls** are messages to other coyotes. _____

7. The high-pitched **sounds** carry three miles or more. _____

8. Fresh game **is** a coyote's favorite food. _____

9. Many **ranchers** complain about coyotes. _____

10. These crafty hunters **steal** newborn livestock. _____

B *Draw a line between the complete subject and complete predicate of each sentence. Underline the simple subject once. Underline the simple predicate twice. The first one is done for you.*

1. Most <u>coyotes</u>|<u>dig</u> underground dens.

2. Their small caves make good homes.

3. These doglike mammals form loose family groups.

4. Most litters contain four to six furry pups.

5. Adults in a group guard the pups.

6. The curious youngsters go on their first hunts at ten weeks of age.

7. Coyotes roam in many American suburbs.

8. Some cities provide enough food for them.

9. The diets of coyotes vary widely.

10. Some survive on insects, fruit, or mice.

11. These timid animals fear humans in the wilderness.

12. They run at the first sight of a person.

C *Choose a complete predicate from the box to complete each sentence. The completed sentences should tell a story about Old Man Coyote. When you finish, underline each simple predicate twice.*

> became much easier   ran from the hunters
>
> kicked sand in the buffalos' eyes   tell a tale about Old Man Coyote
>
> damaged the buffalos' eyesight

1. The Sioux _____

2. Herds of buffalo _____

3. Old Man Coyote _____

4. The sand _____

5. The hunt for buffalo _____

Choose a complete subject from the box to complete each sentence. The completed sentences should tell another story about Old Man Coyote. When you finish, underline each simple subject once.

> One story about Coyote   Old Man Coyote   Bright sunshine
>
> Other Native American tales   The weather

6. _____ describe great deeds of Coyote.

7. _____ tells about a climate change.

8. _____ was always cold and cloudy.

9. _____ moved the sun closer to Earth.

10. _____ heated up the earth.

Online For grammar games and activities, visit
www.grammarworkshop.com.

WRITE

D *Write about a coyote or other animal that lives near your
community. Describe the animal, and tell where and when
you might see it. Tell whether the animal helps or creates problems
for your community.*

"Feathered Coyote" by
Native American artist

_____

_____

_____

_____

_____

_____

_____

_____

_____

_____

_____

_____

_____

_____

_____

Proofreading Checklist ☑

❏ *Does each sentence have a subject and a predicate?*
❏ *Does each sentence begin with a capital letter?*
❏ *Does each sentence have the correct end punctuation?*

Lesson 4: Subjects in Imperative Sentences

LEARN

■ The **subject** of a sentence tells *whom* or *what* the sentence is about.

> **Maria** is dancing in tonight's performance.
> **The ballet** begins at 8:00 P.M.
> **You** should come with us.

■ An **imperative sentence** gives a command or makes a request. The subject of an imperative sentence is always *you*. The word *you* is not stated directly, but it is understood to be the subject.

> **(You)** Please come with us.
> **(You)** Meet us downtown at the theater.

PRACTICE

A *Read each declarative or imperative sentence. For each declarative sentence, write the simple subject. For each imperative sentence, write* **imperative***. Then write* **(You)** *to show the subject of the sentence. The first one is done for you.*

1. Please follow me to our seats. ___imperative (You)___

2. Enjoy the enchanting music. _____

3. You can see the dancers now. _____

4. Ballet began in Italy in the 1400s. _____

5. Feel the joy of these talented performers. _____

6. Notice how graceful they are. _____

7. Most ballerinas begin studying at an early age. _____

8. Many people enjoy the ballet. _____

9. Let yourself go with the music. _____

10. You can glide and spin with the dancers. _____

B *Write the simple subject of each sentence. If the subject is **you understood**, write **(You)**.*

1. This ballet is a story without words. _____

2. The movements tell the story. _____

3. The music helps to tell the story, too. _____

4. Listen to those soft, tuneful notes. _____

5. The youngest ballerina is dancing. _____

6. Hear the loud, scary music. _____

7. An evil villain has come onstage. _____

8. The ballerina's dress is a tutu. _____

9. Watch how easily she moves. _____

10. Those shoes are called pointe shoes. _____

11. Imagine dancing on your toes like that. _____

12. Read more about ballet in this book. _____

13. A choreographer creates the movements in a dance. _____

14. The costumes show the different characters. _____

15. Please share your reaction to the ballet with me. _____

C *Underline the sentence in each item that can be changed to an imperative sentence. Then write the sentence as an imperative. The first one is done for you.*

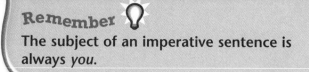

1. Ballet slippers are made of soft leather. <u>You should tie them on tightly.</u>

Tie them on tightly.

2. You must come to class regularly. Keeping up is very important.

3. You must practice all the movements. Your teacher will correct them.

4. The *barre* is the wooden rail against the wall. You can do the exercises there.

5. You must use the proper techniques. Dancers can easily injure their ankles.

6. Dancers practice after a warm-up. You should begin each class with a warm-up.

7. Some classical music is playing now. You should count the beats.

8. You must listen carefully to the rhythm. Dancers count their steps to the music.

9. *The Sleeping Beauty* is a great ballet. You should try to see it soon.

10. Being a dancer takes great energy. You should plan your time carefully.

WRITE

**D** *Write a review about a movie, play, or dance performance that you have seen. Use declarative sentences and imperative sentences in your review. Remember to give the name of the show, and tell whether you would recommend that your friends see it.*

Online For grammar games and activities, visit **www.grammarworkshop.com**.

_____

_____

_____

_____

_____

_____

_____

_____

_____

_____

_____

_____

_____

_____

_____

Proofreading Checklist ✓

❑ *Does each sentence begin with a capital letter?*
❑ *Does each sentence have correct end punctuation?*

Lesson 5: Compound Subjects

LEARN

■ A **compound subject** has two or more simple subjects that share the same predicate. The subjects are joined by the word *and* or *or*.

<u>Homes</u> **and** <u>businesses</u> need energy.
<u>Petroleum</u>, <u>coal</u>, **and** <u>natural gas</u> are fossil fuels.
The <u>sun</u> **or** <u>wind</u> could provide our energy.

■ A **conjunction** is a word that joins words or groups of words. In a compound subject, the conjunction *and* or *or* joins the subjects.

■ If two related sentences have the same predicate, you can combine the sentences by joining the subjects with the conjunction *and* or *or*. The new sentence will have a compound subject.

<u>Cars</u> run on petroleum. <u>Trucks</u> run on petroleum.
<u>Cars</u> **and** <u>trucks</u> run on petroleum.

PRACTICE

A *Each sentence below has a compound subject. Only one of the simple subjects in the compound subject is underlined. Write the other simple subject (or subjects) on the line provided. The first one is done for you.*

1. <u>Oil</u>, coal, and gas were formed in the ground. _____coal, gas_____

2. <u>Animals</u> and plants died millions of years ago. _____

3. Intense <u>heat</u> and pressure slowly turned them into fossil fuels. _____

4. <u>Scientists</u> or engineers might find these underground fuels. _____

5. Coal mines and <u>oil wells</u> are found in many places. _____

6. <u>Texas</u> and Alaska produce some of our fossil fuel. _____

7. Tanks or <u>pipelines</u> transport these fuels. _____

8. Many <u>homes</u> and buildings are heated with gas. _____

9. Ink, <u>crayons</u>, and bubble gum are all made from oil. _____

10. <u>Tires</u>, CDs, and detergents also come from oil. _____

B *In each sentence, underline the simple subjects in the compound subject. Then write the conjunction that joins the simple subjects. The first one is done for you.*

1. The <u>sun</u> and its <u>rays</u> provide Earth with energy. _____ **and** _____

2. The heat and light make life on Earth possible. _____

3. All trees and plants need sunlight to grow. _____

4. People and animals depend on plants for food. _____

5. Sunshine and light affect our moods and feelings. _____

6. Cloudy days and dark nights tend to be gloomy times. _____

7. A bright morning or sunny day cheers us up. _____

8. Houses and cars feel too hot in summer. _____

9. Children and adults might get a sunburn at the beach. _____

10. Hair, eyes, or skin can be harmed by too much sun. _____

11. Scientists and engineers look for ways to use the sun's energy. _____

12. New inventions and improvements are needed. _____

C *Choose a simple subject from the box to complete each sentence. The word or words you choose will complete the compound subject in each sentence.*

 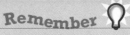
> blades   businesses   farmers   gust   I   sheep   wheat

1. My parents and _____ visited a wind farm.

2. Many _____ and ranchers place windmills in their fields.

3. Cattle or _____ graze among the giant structures.

4. Corn or _____ grows around them.

5. A _____ or steady breeze turns the windmill's blades.

6. These _____ and gears create electricity.

7. Homeowners and _____ buy the electric power.

> cities   fields   Great Plains   mountains   wind farms

8. Most _____ and hills get a lot of wind.

9. The prairies and _____ are windy, too.

10. Windmills and _____ are common in these areas.

11. Towns or _____ have no wind farms.

12. Big open areas or _____ are hard to find in cities.

Wind farm

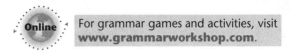

WRITE

D *Remember that two related sentences with the same predicate can be combined. The subject of the new sentence is the compound subject formed by combining the subjects of the two sentences. The predicate is the predicate that the sentences have in common. In each item below, underline the two sentences that can be combined. Use the conjunction in parentheses to combine the subjects. Then write the new sentence on the line. The first one is done for you.*

1. <u>My friends walk places whenever possible.</u> Saving energy is important. <u>I walk places whenever possible.</u> (and)

   My friends and I walk places whenever possible.

2. Make your home energy efficient. Leaky faucets waste energy. Open windows waste energy. (and)

   _____

3. Heating a house is expensive. Heavy drapes can lower heating costs. Clean furnace ducts can lower heating costs. (or)

   _____

4. My parents turn off lights to save electricity. Most electricity comes from fossil fuels. I turn off lights to save electricity. (or)

   _____

5. Heating water uses energy. Running full dishwashers saves hot water. Taking shorter showers saves hot water. (and)

   _____

Go back to the sentences you wrote.
Circle the compound subject in each sentence.

Lesson 6: Compound Predicates

LEARN

- A **compound predicate** has two or more simple predicates that share the same subject. The predicates are joined by the conjunction *and* or *or*.

    Many Americans <u>read</u> **and** <u>write</u> e-mail on computers.
    We <u>use</u> **or** <u>interact</u> with computers in many ways.

- If two related sentences have the same subject, you can combine the sentences by joining the predicates with the conjunction *and* or *or*. The new sentence will have a compound predicate.

    Students <u>research</u> information online.
    Students <u>download</u> information online.
    Students <u>research</u> **and** <u>download</u> information online.

    Shoppers <u>browse</u> online.
    Shoppers <u>order</u> merchandise online.
    Shoppers <u>browse</u> **or** <u>order</u> merchandise online.

PRACTICE

A *Each sentence below has a compound predicate. Only one of the simple predicates in the compound predicate is underlined. Write the other simple predicate on the line. The first one is done for you.*

1. Computers <u>change</u> and improve our lives.   _____improve_____

2. In classrooms, computers teach or <u>review</u> skills.   _____

3. Emilio <u>studies</u> and writes on his computer.   _____

4. Many people <u>chat</u> or listen to music online.   _____

5. Friends send and <u>share</u> photos.   _____

6. People buy or <u>sell</u> things over the Internet.   _____

7. Businesses <u>protect</u> and save their files.   _____

8. Library computers describe and <u>locate</u> books.   _____

9. In stores, computers <u>complete</u> and record sales.   _____

10. The computers in ATMs read and <u>accept</u> bankcards.   _____

B *In each sentence, underline the simple predicates in the compound predicate. Then write the conjunction that joins the simple predicates.*

1. Many people buy or rent computer games.   _____

2. Our class visited and toured a computer game company.   _____

3. We met and talked with the workers.   _____

4. The workers discuss and plan a new game for a long time.   _____

5. An artist draws and outlines a storyboard for the game.   _____

6. The storyboard shows and explains each scene in the game.   _____

7. A good game grabs and holds a player's attention.   _____

8. A sports game looks and sounds realistic.   _____

9. Skilled artists model or draw the action in each scene.   _____

10. Other workers write and test the game's software.   _____

11. Software runs and displays a game on a computer or a game machine.   _____

12. Finally, the company advertises and sells its game.   _____

C *Choose a simple predicate from the box to complete each sentence. The word you choose will complete the compound predicate in each sentence.*

designed	divided	needed	simplified	subtracts	used

1. Ancient Middle Eastern traders invented and

_____ the abacus.

2. An abacus adds or _____
numbers quickly.

Abacus

3. Some people multiplied or _____
using an abacus.

4. During the 1800s, businesses wanted and _____
calculating machines.

5. Many inventors _____ and built mechanical calculators.

6. Engineers gradually improved and _____ these machines.

demonstrated	developed	impressed	installed	published	weighed

7. In the 1840s, Charles Babbage wrote and _____ his plans
for a computer.

8. Babbage never built or _____ his invention.

9. In the 1940s, the U.S. Army funded and _____ an
electronic computer called ENIAC.

10. ENIAC filled a room and _____ 30 tons.

11. ENIAC surprised and _____ everyone.

12. Many businesses bought and _____ huge new computers.

 **WRITE**

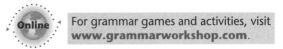
Online | For grammar games and activities, visit www.grammarworkshop.com.

D *Remember that two related sentences with the same subject can be combined. The subject of the new sentence is the subject that the sentences have in common. The predicate is the compound predicate formed by combining the predicates of the two sentences. In each item below, underline the two sentences that can be combined. Use the conjunction in parentheses to combine the predicates. Then write the new sentence on the line. The first one is done for you.*

1. Computers got smaller in the 1960s. <u>Scientists invented computer chips.</u> <u>Scientists installed computer chips.</u> (and)

   Scientists invented and installed computer chips.

2. Some companies designed desktop computers. Some companies sold desktop computers. In the 1970s, businesses bought these smaller computers. (or)

3. Consumers leased the small computers. Consumers bought the small computers. Popular programs for "personal computers" appeared during the 1980s. (or)

4. The World Wide Web began in the 1990s. Home computer users liked the Web. Home computer users used the Web. (and)

5. Computer experts designed tiny computers. Computer experts produced tiny computers. These hand-held devices became immensely popular. (and)

 Go back to the sentences you wrote. Circle the compound predicate in each sentence.

Lesson 7: **Compound Sentences**

LEARN

■ A **simple sentence** has one subject and one predicate.
It expresses one complete idea.

> The Vikings lived in Scandinavia 1000 years ago.

Andevan Bronzeworks, Inc.

■ A **compound sentence** combines two simple sentences
that have related ideas. A conjunction (*and, but,* or *or*)
joins the two sentences. Always use a comma before the
conjunction in a compound sentence.

- Use *and* to join two related sentences that are alike
  in some way.

  > Vikings were fine sailors, **and** they had the best
  > ships in the world.

- Use *but* to join two related sentences that show a contrast.

  > The Vikings were early explorers, **but** they were raiders, too.

- Use *or* to join two related sentences that show a choice.

  > Vikings sailed their longboats, **or** they rowed their ships.

PRACTICE

A *Underline the two simple sentences in each compound sentence. If the
sentence is not a compound sentence, write **not compound**.*

1. Most Vikings were farmers, but good farmland
was scarce.   _____

2. These Scandinavians raided nearby lands for riches.   _____

3. Vikings sailed by the stars, or they followed the
shoreline.   _____

4. Some warships were almost 100 feet long.   _____

5. The Vikings were fierce fighters, and other
Europeans feared them.   _____

6. Vikings burned entire villages during their raids.   _____

7. Vikings first raided England, but they soon reached
Italy and Spain.   _____

8. The Vikings described their adventures in long tales
called sagas   _____

9. Vikings were raiders at first, but they became traders later.   _____

10. They established forts and colonies along their
trade routes.   _____

B *Read each incomplete compound sentence. Underline the sentence below
that best relates to it. Then combine the related sentences to form a
compound sentence. Write the compound sentence on the line.*

1. The Vikings were daring explorers, and ____.
They grew oats and rye on small farms. They bravely sailed across the Atlantic.

_____

2. The Vikings explored Iceland and Greenland, and ____.
Thousands of them settled there. Vikings wrote messages with letters called *runes*.

_____

3. The Vikings established Vinland in North America, but ____.
Their colony lasted only a few years. The colonists hunted reindeer and seals.

_____

4. The Vikings abandoned Vinland, or ____.
They might have died from disease or attack. Viking forts were built with wood.

_____

5. The Atlantic voyages were long and dangerous, but ____.
The Vikings loved exploring. The Vikings became successful traders.

_____

C *Read this section of Jon's report about Viking ships. He made five mistakes in the compound sentences he wrote. Find the mistakes, and use the proofreading marks to correct them.*

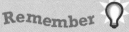

Remember

A **compound sentence** is formed by joining two simple sentences with a conjunction such as *and*, *or*, or *but*. Always use a comma before the conjunction.

Viking ships were built from wood. Most of them rotted away long ago, but a few have survived. Viking chiefs were buried in the ground or they were buried in their ships. Several burial ships have been found.

In 1880, a Viking ship was dug up in Gokstad in Norway. The ship is 76 feet long but it measures only 17 feet across. You can see why the Viking ships are called "longboats." An exact copy of this ship once sailed from Norway to Canada. The craft steered easily and it held up well in fierce storms.

Another Viking ship was dug up in Oseberg in 1906. This craft is smaller than the Gokstad ship but it has many more decorative carvings. The Oseberg ship might have been used in raids, or it might have belonged to a Viking queen.

Viking ships were "clinker built." This means that the boards of the ship overlap each other. The ships were very strong and they were also light and graceful.

Proofreading Marks

∧	Add
⊙	Period
ℐ	Take out
≡	Capital letter
/	Small letter

Did you correct five mistakes in the compound sentences?

Online — For grammar games and activities, visit
www.grammarworkshop.com.

WRITE

D *Each pair of sentences contains related ideas. Combine the sentences to make a compound sentence. Use the conjunction **and, but,** or **or** to combine them. Remember to put a comma before the conjunction.*

1. A Viking house might have a stone foundation. Its walls and roof were made of sod.

_____

_____

2. A Viking warrior might fight with an ax. He might use a sword.

_____

_____

3. Eric the Red might be the best known Viking explorer. Leif Ericson might have that honor.

_____

_____

4. The Viking Age lasted about 300 years. By 1100, the fierce raids had ended.

_____

_____

5. The Vikings established trade routes in Europe. They built market towns and ports.

_____

_____

6. The Vikings told stories about their gods and heroes. We still read these myths today.

_____

_____

Lesson 8: **Complex Sentences**

LEARN

- A **complex sentence** is made up of two related ideas joined by a **subordinating conjunction**.

The following subordinating conjunctions are often used to connect the related ideas.

Subordinating Conjunctions			
after	although	because	before
since	until	when	while

- You can combine two sentences with related ideas to form a complex sentence.

> Safety tips are useful. They prevent accidents.
> Safety tips are useful **because** they prevent accidents.

> Ed rides his bike. He wears a helmet.
> **When** Ed rides his bike, he wears a helmet.

Notice that when the first idea begins with a subordinating conjunction, a comma follows that idea.

PRACTICE

A *Read each sentence. Write **complex** if the sentence is made up of two related ideas joined by a subordinating conjunction. Write **not complex** if it is not a complex sentence. Circle the subordinating conjunction in each complex sentence.*

1. Gary does warm-up exercises before he jogs. _____

2. After he finishes his run, he puts on a sweat suit. _____

3. Lisa bikes on the right side of the road since it is safer. _____

4. She obeys all traffic signals while she rides. _____

5. Marie walks home from school every day. _____

6. When the weather is nice, she walks three miles a day. _____

7. Marie finishes her walk early today. _____

8. Carla wears a life jacket in her canoe although she can swim. _____

9. She keeps the life jacket on until she is back on shore. _____

10. Because Ellen spends time in the sun, she wears sunscreen. _____

B *Underline the two related ideas in each complex sentence. Write the subordinating conjunction that joins them. The first one is done for you.*

1. Although <u>many accidents occur at home</u>, <u>most people feel safe there</u>.   _____Although_____

2. The kitchen is especially risky since it is so busy. _____

3. Keep kitchen equipment in a safe place until you need it. _____

4. Put away mops and brooms after you clean the floor. _____

5. Be careful near the stove because foods are very hot. _____

6. While your foods cook, turn pot handles toward the back of the stove. _____

7. Since falls can occur in the bathroom, you must be careful there. _____

8. Put down a nonskid rug before you take a shower or bath. _____

9. Before you climb a ladder, make sure it is steady. _____

10. When you use fertilizers or sprays, wear gloves and a mask. _____

11. Put away all tools before someone trips over them. _____

12. Your home will be safer when you take safety seriously. _____

C *Write a subordinating conjunction to complete each sentence. Choose a subordinating conjunction from the box, or use a subordinating conjunction of your own.*

 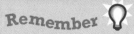
after	although	because	before
since	until	when	while

1. _____ winter sports are fun, they can be dangerous, too.

2. Several layers of clothes keep you warm _____ you are out in the cold.

3. _____ your head and hands lose heat quickly, wear a hat and a pair of gloves.

4. Never skate on ice _____ it is frozen solid.

5. Don't go on the ice _____ officials check its safety.

6. _____ trees can be a danger, choose an open area for sledding.

7. Swimmers must be careful _____ water accidents are common.

8. A lifeguard should be on duty _____ you go swimming.

9. Don't go in the water _____ at least one other swimmer is with you.

10. Don't stay in the water alone _____ everyone has left.

11. _____ thunderstorms are nearby, stay out of the water.

12. Watch young children carefully _____ they are in the water.

Online — For grammar games and activities, visit www.grammarworkshop.com.

WRITE

D *Write a complex sentence by adding a related idea either before or after each item. Write the sentence on the line. Remember to put a comma after the first idea if it starts with a subordinating conjunction. The first one is done for you.*

1. because accidents can happen in a second <u>Because accidents can happen in a</u>

<u>second, everyone needs to stay alert. *Or:* Everyone needs to stay alert because</u>

<u>accidents can happen in a second.</u>

2. when objects are left in the aisles _____

_____

3. until the fire drill is over _____

_____

4. when you play in the gym _____

_____

5. before you cross the street _____

_____

6. since the steps are slippery _____

_____

7. while you go up and down stairs _____

_____

8. although you might be late for class _____

_____

Proofreading Checklist ✔

❏ *Does each complex sentence contain two related ideas?*
❏ *Does each complex sentence use a subordinating conjunction to join the two ideas?*

Lesson 9: **Fragments and Run-ons**

LEARN

■ A **fragment** is an incomplete sentence. To correct
a fragment, add the missing subject or predicate.

FRAGMENT   Come in small packages. (missing a subject)
SENTENCE   Good things come in small packages.

■ A **run-on sentence** is two sentences that run together. To
correct a run-on sentence, write two separate sentences or
write a compound sentence.

RUN-ON
You can lead a horse to water you cannot
make it drink.

TWO SENTENCES
You can lead a horse to water. You cannot
make it drink.

COMPOUND SENTENCE
You can lead a horse to water, **but** you
cannot make it drink.

■ A run-on sentence with only a comma between the two
sentences is called a **comma splice**. Correct a comma splice
by writing a compound sentence or two separate sentences.

RUN-ON
Sticks and stones may break my bones, words will never hurt me.

COMPOUND SENTENCE
Sticks and stones may break my bones, **but** words will never
hurt me.

PRACTICE

A *Write **sentence, fragment,** or **run-on** to describe each group of words.
Write **comma splice** if the run-on is a comma splice.*

1. A needle in a haystack.   _____

2. Two heads are better than one.   _____

3. Is always greener on the other side.   _____

4. Running the race isn't enough you have to start on time. _____

5. The best things in life. _____

6. Money isn't everything. _____

7. Some people are masters of money, others are its slaves. _____

8. Worth a thousand words. _____

9. You can put a silk coat on a goat, it's still a goat. _____

10. Nobody is perfect. _____

B *Make each fragment a complete sentence by matching it to the correct subject or predicate.*

1. A proverb   **a.** contain simple and colorful language.

2. Most proverbs   **b.** sums up a simple truth.

3. Every culture   **c.** has its own proverbs.

4. To become a proverb, a saying   **d.** must be used for a long time.

Correct each run-on sentence. Write two separate sentences or a compound sentence.

5. The meaning of most proverbs is obvious some are puzzling.

_____

6. A proverb can give us insight, it might teach a value.

_____

7. Students once copied long lists of proverbs they memorized them.

_____

8. Look for proverbs online, the library has dictionaries of proverbs.

_____

C *Anna wrote a story about her first day at school. In these paragraphs from the story, she wrote five run-on sentences. Use the proofreading marks to correct the run-ons.*

 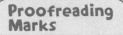
It was my first day of fifth grade in a new school. "I wish I still went to Valley School," I told Mom. The thought of a new school excited me it also frightened me.

"The grass is always greener on the other side of the fence," Mom replied. I gave her a blank stare. I wondered why Mom was talking about grass and fences.

Mom handed me my jacket. "You'd better hurry, you'll miss the bus. Time and tide wait for no one." Again I stared at her. I had plenty of time, the ocean was 100 miles away.

"A journey of a thousand miles begins with a single step," Mom said as she kissed me good-bye. I headed out the door. The school was only two miles away Mom and I both knew that.

A sea of strange faces stared at me as I climbed onto the bus. I smiled at them all I was going to make the best of it. I told myself, "Today is the first day of the rest of my life!"

Proofreading Marks	
∧	Add
⊙	Period
ℓ	Take out
≡	Capital letter
/	Small letter

Did you correct five run-on sentences?

1000 MILE JOURNEY

Online For grammar games and activities, visit
www.grammarworkshop.com.

WRITE

D *Add a subject or predicate to each fragment, and rewrite it as a complete sentence. Try to write a familiar or an original proverb.*

1. an apple a day _____

_____

2. is the best policy _____

_____

3. a journey of a thousand miles _____

_____

4. always climbs higher the next time _____

_____

5. can move mountains _____

_____

6. must come to an end _____

_____

7. the mighty oak tree _____

_____

8. wasted time _____

_____

9. is my enemy _____

_____

10. people in glass houses _____

_____

Kinds of Sentences (pp. 8–11) *Read each sentence, and add an end mark. Write* **declarative, interrogative, imperative,** *or* **exclamatory** *to tell what kind of sentence it is.*

1. Are we in Arizona's Petrified Forest _____   _____

2. This national park contains petrified wood _____   _____

3. How gigantic and beautiful the stone logs are _____   _____

Complete Subjects and Predicates (pp. 12–15) *Read each sentence. Underline the complete subject once. Underline the complete predicate twice.*

4. This area was a wetland millions of years ago.

5. The huge trees died from disease or insects.

6. Many trees fell into muddy water.

Simple Subjects and Predicates (pp. 16–19) *Read each sentence. Underline the simple subject once. Underline the simple predicate twice.*

7. The swampy mud contained many minerals.

8. The old logs absorbed these minerals gradually.

9. The different minerals gave the stone bright colors.

Subjects in Imperative Sentences (pp. 20–23) *Read each declarative or imperative sentence. Write the simple subject of each declarative sentence. Write* **(You)** *to show the subject of each imperative sentence.*

10. Look at this display over here.   _____

11. These changes occurred 200 million years ago.   _____

12. You can see the layers of mud and sand.   _____

Compound Subjects (pp. 24–27) *Underline the simple subjects in each compound subject.*

13. The geography and climate changed gradually.

14. Wind and rain uncovered the buried stone logs.

15. The logs and fossils came into view.

Compound Predicates (pp. 28–31) *Underline the simple predicates in each compound predicate.*

16. Many tourists visit and photograph the Painted Desert.

17. The Painted Desert rolls and stretches across much of northern Arizona.

18. Bright sands shimmer and shine in the sun.

Compound Sentences (pp. 32–35) *Underline the conjunction that joins the two sentences in each compound sentence.*

19. The Navajo people have lived in this desert for 1000 years, and the Hopi have lived here, too.

20. This landscape seems ancient, but it is constantly changing.

21. You might see dinosaur tracks here, or you might find fossils of prehistoric plants.

Complex Sentences (pp. 36–39) *Underline the subordinating conjunction in each complex sentence.*

22. Spanish explorers named this the Painted Desert because it had such bright colors.

23. Although the desert is beautiful at sunset, sunrise is amazing, too.

24. The Navajo dig up the desert's red clay since it is ideal for pottery.

Fragments and Run-ons (pp. 40–43) *Write **sentence, fragment,** or **run-on** to describe each group of words.*

25. Most of the Painted Desert lies within the Navajo nation. _____

26. Visit the Painted Desert, you won't be disappointed. _____

27. One of our country's most amazing natural areas. _____

DIRECTIONS *Fill in the circle next to the sentence that has correct capitalization and punctuation. The first one is done for you.*

1. ○ Who visits your house six days a week.

   ● Think about it.

   ○ Your letter carrier delivers mail Monday through Saturday

   ○ How great it is to receive a letter or package.

2. ○ How many post office workers are there.

   ○ More than 700,000 people work for the post office.

   ○ Wow, that's a lot of people

   ○ Mail carriers walk or they drive vehicles to deliver the mail.

3. ○ Tell me more about the U.S. Postal Service

   ○ there are 38,000 post offices.

   ○ Must deliver to all parts of the city.

   ○ Read this article about what they do.

4. ○ The post office has many workers, it delivers so much mail.

   ○ How much mail does it deliver in a year.

   ○ The amount varies, but it's over 210 billion items a year.

   ○ Did you say *billion*

5. ○ Our postal service handles 44 percent of the world's mail.

   ○ That's a huge amount of mail

   ○ Almost eight million Americans go to the post office every day, more use mailboxes.

   ○ Does that surprise you.

6. ○ Post office workers once sorted mail by hand

   ○ What a difficult job that must have been?

   ○ Introduced a system of ZIP codes.

   ○ High-speed machines now sort the mail, and delivery times are faster.

7. ○ some machines sort 60,000 letters an hour.

   ○ Wow, that's amazing

   ○ How do they do it.

   ○ The machine prints a code on the envelope after it scans the address.

8. ○ Postal workers stop at 144 million addresses every day

   ○ Many postal workers are on the job while we sleep.

   ○ We take the mail for granted but, it's very important.

   ○ Have you thanked your letter carrier recently.

DIRECTIONS *Read the paragraphs, and look carefully at each underlined part. Fill in the circle next to the answer choice that shows the correct capitalization and punctuation. If the underlined part is already correct, fill in the circle for "Correct as is." The first one is done for you.*

How did people send <u>letters before there was a post office.</u> Usually, they
(9)
didn't. Long ago, few people could <u>read, they</u> didn't write letters. Wealthy
(10)
people hired <u>messengers when</u> they sent letters.
(11)

The United States declared independence <u>in 1776 and it</u> set up a postal system
(12)
right away. Benjamin Franklin was named the first postmaster. What a good

choice <u>he was the</u> clever Franklin mapped and organized delivery routes. More
(13)
and more Americans <u>sent, and received mail, because</u> of Franklin's leadership.
(14)

9. ○ letters, before there was a post office.

  ● letters before there was a post office?

  ○ letters before, there was a post office?

  ○ Correct as is

10. ○ read. and they

  ○ read and, they

  ○ read, and they

  ○ Correct as is

11. ○ messengers. When

  ○ messengers, and when

  ○ messengers, when

  ○ Correct as is

12. ○ in 1776, it

  ○ in 1776. and it

  ○ in 1776, and it

  ○ Correct as is

13. ○ he was, the

  ○ he was? The

  ○ he was! The

  ○ Correct as is

14. ○ sent and received mail because

  ○ sent and received mail. Because

  ○ sent, and received mail because

  ○ Correct as is

Lesson 10: Common and Proper Nouns

LEARN

- A **noun** is a word that names a person, place, or thing.

  NOUNS　athlete　　town　　race

  Many **athletes** came to our **town** for the **race**.

Nouns can also name things you cannot see, such as ideas.

  NOUNS　happiness　challenge　freedom　excitement

  The **challenge** and **excitement** brought them here.

- A **proper noun** names a specific person, place, thing, or idea. Capitalize all the important words in a proper noun. A noun that does not name a specific person, place, thing, or idea is a **common noun**. Common nouns are not capitalized.

Common Nouns	Proper Nouns
people	Max Gallo, Stacey Lee Jones
city or town	Chicago, Baton Rouge
states	California, North Carolina
countries	Japan, Spain
continents	North America, Asia
lakes, oceans, mountains	Tule Lake, Atlantic Ocean
	Rocky Mountains
buildings	White House, Hillsdale School
special events	Cape Five-Mile Run, Olympic Games
months, days, holidays	May, Sunday, Fourth of July

PRACTICE

*Write **common** or **proper** to describe each noun. If the noun is a proper noun, capitalize it and write it correctly.*

1. florida　　　　　　　　　　　　　　　＿＿＿＿＿＿＿＿＿＿＿＿＿＿

2. mountain　　　　　　　　　　　　　　＿＿＿＿＿＿＿＿＿＿＿＿＿＿

3. asia　　　　　　　　　　　　　　　　＿＿＿＿＿＿＿＿＿＿＿＿＿＿

4. statue of liberty _____

5. hospital _____

6. boston marathon _____

7. sadness _____

8. blue ridge mountains _____

9. intelligence _____

10. tenth avenue _____

B *Find the two nouns in each sentence. Underline the noun if it is a common noun. Circle the noun if it is a proper noun, and write it correctly on the line. The first one is done for you.*

1. Unusual <u>races</u> occur all over the (united states). ⟶ **United States**

2. The denver gorilla run is a funny event. _____

3. All contestants dress as gorillas. _____

4. They raise money for a conservation fund. _____

5. These animals are endangered in africa. _____

6. A very muddy competition occurs in washington. _____

7. Its official name is the samish bay low tide mud run. _____

8. The pacific ocean is the beautiful backdrop. _____

9. The athletes must trudge through thick mud. _____

10. This contest supports education. _____

11. Another unusual race takes place at the north pole. _____

12. The marathoners race across the frozen arctic ocean. _____

C *Read this entry from Regina's journal. Regina didn't capitalize three proper nouns. She also capitalized eight common nouns by mistake. Use the proofreading marks to correct the errors.*

Remember 💡
A **proper noun** names a specific person, place, thing, or idea. Begin each important word in a proper noun with a capital letter.

When sally said the Boat races at Heber Springs would be interesting, I believed her. I just didn't know how interesting! Today, Sally's parents drove us there from Little Rock, and I couldn't believe it.

All 50 boats on the Water were made from cardboard! Many were over 40 feet long. One looked like a Battleship. Another was modeled after a spaceship. There was even a boat that looked like a Chicken!

You could see Enthusiasm and Pride in the faces of the racers. Some had spent months designing and building their boats. They had come from all over arkansas, other States, and canada.

The crowd cheered when the Race began. Sailors paddled madly around the 200-yard course. Each hoped to win the top prize.

Proofreading Marks	
∧	Add
⊙	Period
ℒ	Take out
≡	Capital letter
/	Small letter

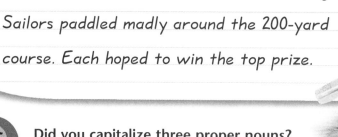

Did you capitalize three proper nouns?
Did you lowercase eight common nouns?

WRITE

D *Proper nouns can make your writing more interesting and more exact. Change the words in **boldface** in each sentence to a proper noun. Write the new sentence. You may use the names of real people, places, and things, or you may make up names. The first one is done for you.*

1. **A friend** and I might organize a funny race.

Marla and I might organize a funny race.

2. This event would raise money to clean **the pond**.

_____

3. Maybe **a teacher** would help us plan the details.

_____

4. Let's have a meeting at **the library**.

_____

5. We could hold the race in **a park**.

_____

6. Maybe we could run the race on **a street**.

_____

7. Many students at **the school** might take part.

_____

8. **A holiday** might be a good day for the race.

_____

9. A day in **a spring month** would be the best time.

_____

10. Let's put up signs all over **the town**.

_____

Lesson 11: Singular and Plural Nouns

LEARN

- A noun that names one person, place, thing, or idea is a **singular noun**. A noun that names more than one person, place, thing, or idea is a **plural noun**.

SINGULAR	This **penguin** lives in the Arctic.
PLURAL	A group of **penguins** huddle together to keep warm.

- Form the plural of most singular nouns by adding -s.

SINGULAR	mountain	river	rock	idea
PLURAL	mountain**s**	river**s**	rock**s**	idea**s**

- Form the plural of nouns ending in s, ss, x, ch, or sh by adding -es.

SINGULAR	gas	class	tax	peach	brush
PLURAL	gas**es**	class**es**	tax**es**	peach**es**	brush**es**

- Form the plural of nouns ending with a vowel and y by adding -s.

SINGULAR	alley	day	toy
PLURAL	alley**s**	day**s**	toy**s**

- Form the plural of nouns ending with a consonant and y by changing the y to i and adding -es.

SINGULAR	city	party	berry
PLURAL	cit**ies**	part**ies**	berr**ies**

PRACTICE

A *Write the plural form of each noun.*

1. cherry _____

2. turkey _____

3. dish _____

4. stitch _____

5. vegetable _____

6. bus _____

7. pass _____

8. box _____

9. enemy _____

10. lake _____

B *In each sentence, one of the nouns in **boldface** should be plural. Circle the noun, and write it correctly. The first one is done for you.*

1. The Arctic is a cold **region** stretching across three (**continent**).   continents

2. The northern **border** of Europe, Asia, and North America form this **land**.   _____

3. The North Pole, Greenland, and many **island** lie in the **area**.   _____

4. This chilly **landscape** has no large **city**.   _____

5. A **traveler** can visit many small **community**.   _____

6. Winter **month** are dark in this cold **place**.   _____

7. Bright green **patch** cover the **ground**.   _____

8. The southern Arctic is an **area** with many different **grass**.   _____

9. Different **moss** grow in this swampy **region**.   _____

10. Small **bush**, no taller than a **bicycle**, are common.   _____

11. Some **valley** are filled with plant **life**.   _____

12. During warm **weather**, even **berry** ripen.   _____

13. Arctic **mine** produce **gold** and copper.   _____

14. Oil **company** pump oil from the frozen **ground**.   _____

15. This natural **resource** attracts **explorer** to the Arctic.   _____

C Ellen wrote a report about Arctic wildlife. She made nine mistakes when writing plural nouns. Sometimes she misspelled plural nouns. At other times, she used a plural noun for a singular noun or a singular noun for a plural noun. Use the proofreading marks in the box to correct these mistakes.

Proofreading Marks

∧	Add
⊙	Period
✎	Take out
≡	Capital letter
/	Small letter

The Arctic is a hard places to live, but many animals survive there. In spring, swarms of flys, bees, and other insects fill the air. Flocks of ducks and other birds nest in the Arctic. Most arrive in June, flying north from warmer territorys.

Lemmings and voles are animals that live in the Arctic. These tiny mouselike animals eat the many different grass that grow here. In turn, owles and foxs prey on the lemmings. Arctic animals raise large familys when food is plentiful.

Seals also live in the Arctic. Whole colonys of seals feed on the plentiful sea life. There are also walruss. They use their tusks to dig clams and worms from the sea floor. Whales and dolphins also move north into the Arctic sea when the ice of winter breaks up.

Did you correct nine errors?

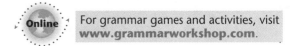

Online For grammar games and activities, visit **www.grammarworkshop.com**.

WRITE

D Choose a set of nouns in one of the boxes. Write a few sentences that tell a story. Use your imagination to make up your story. Include the plural form of most of the nouns in the box.

iceberg	fox	mountain
walrus	grass	valley
polar bear	berry	grizzly
seal	owl	hunter
home	fish	bush

_____

_____

_____

_____

_____

_____

_____

_____

_____

_____

_____

Proofreading Checklist ☑

❏ *Did you write sentences using the plural forms of the nouns in the box?*
❏ *Did you follow the rules for spelling these plural nouns?*

Lesson 12: **Irregular Plural Nouns**

LEARN

Some nouns have **irregular plurals**. There are special rules for forming these plurals.

- For some nouns ending in *f* or *fe*, change the *f* to *v* and add *-es*. For other nouns ending in *f* or *fe*, add *-s*.

SINGULAR	leaf	life	roof
PLURAL	lea**ves**	li**ves**	roof**s**

- For nouns ending in a vowel and *o*, add *-s*.

SINGULAR	video	radio	studio
PLURAL	video**s**	radio**s**	studio**s**

- For nouns ending in a consonant and *o*, add *-s* to some nouns. Add *-es* to other nouns.

SINGULAR	piano	hero	tomato
PLURAL	piano**s**	hero**es**	tomato**es**

- Some nouns have a special form that does not end in *-s*.

SINGULAR	foot	woman	tooth	child	goose
PLURAL	feet	women	teeth	children	geese

- Some nouns stay the same in the singular and plural forms.

SINGULAR	deer	sheep	moose
PLURAL	deer	sheep	moose

PRACTICE

A *Write the plural form of each noun. You may use a dictionary to check the plural forms.*

1. rodeo _____

2. loaf _____

3. knife _____

4. mouse _____

5. scarf _____

6. potato _____

7. cuff _____

8. man _____

9. foot _____

10. moose _____

B *In each item, one of the nouns in **boldface** should be plural. Circle the noun that should be plural, and write it correctly. You may use a dictionary to check the plural forms.*

1. Why was I late for **school** today?
   Two **tornado** blew me away! _____

2. The first one touched down near the **zoo**.
   You should have seen those **kangaroo**! _____

3. I ran as fast as my **foot** would go.
   I had to outrun a **buffalo**. _____

4. A dozen **auto** were up on a **roof**.
   It's true although I don't have proof. _____

5. Husbands and **wife** were bouncing around.
   Even a **rhino** couldn't stay on the ground. _____

6. At the market, I dodged a bag of **potato**.
   I slipped and fell on a **tomato**. _____

7. The food from that **store** whirled here and there.
   I saw bananas and **loaf** of bread in the air. _____

8. Then a second twister hit the **town**.
   Two **woman** shouted, "Get down, get down!" _____

9. You didn't see that **cyclone** hit?
   The other **schoolchild** didn't spot it? _____

10. You think my story is an **excuse**?
    You think there were no flying **moose**? _____

11. There was no news about it on the **radio**?
    Nobody snapped any **photo**? _____

12. Well, then maybe it wasn't a **tornado**.
    Maybe I got caught in two **volcano**. _____

C *During a car trip, Ava read these signs along the road. She counted eight plural nouns that were spelled incorrectly. Use the proofreading marks to correct the mistakes in the signs.*

Remember 💡
Irregular nouns form their plurals in special ways. Learn the rules for forming the plurals of these nouns.

1.
Farmer's Market
Fresh Corn, Tomatos, and Potatoes

2.
Attention Drivers
Watch out for
Moose and Deers

Proofreading Marks

∧	Add
⊙	Period
ℰ	Take out
≡	Capital letter
/	Small letter

3.
Buckle Up
Seat Belts Save Lifes

4.
All-Season
Construction Company
Decks, Basements, Rooves

5.
Family Dentistry
We're Nice to Your Teeth

6.
CAUTION!!!
Ducks and Gooses Cross Here

7.
Bob's
Video Rentals
Home of 50,000 Videoes

8.
War Heroes Memorial
2 Miles

9.
Low Bridge Ahead
Maximum Height
12 Foot

10.
Supreme Movers
Pianoes Are Our Specialty

LOOK Back Did you correct the spelling of eight plural nouns?

WRITE

D *Write the plural forms of the nouns in each pair. Then write a sentence using both plural nouns. The first one is done for you.*

1. man _____ men _____   woman _____ women _____

  The men and women enjoyed the concert. _____

2. calf _____   child _____

  _____

3. deer _____   leaf _____

  _____

4. bush _____   moose _____

  _____

5. potato _____   knife _____

  _____

6. bookshelf _____   video _____

  _____

7. sheep _____   tooth _____

  _____

8. echo _____   piano _____

  _____

9. photo _____   goose _____

  _____

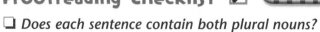

Proofreading Checklist ✓

❑ *Does each sentence contain both plural nouns?*
❑ *Are the plural forms spelled correctly?*

Lesson 13: **Possessive Nouns**

LEARN

A **possessive noun** is a noun that shows ownership
or possession.

> **Rosa's** family works in the community garden.
> Her **family's** garden has flowers and vegetables.
> Many **families'** vegetables are ripe now.

- To make a singular noun possessive, add an
  apostrophe and -*s*.

SINGULAR	Rosa	family
SINGULAR POSSESSIVE	Rosa's	family's

- To make a plural noun that ends in -*s* possessive,
  add only an apostrophe.

PLURAL	families	students
PLURAL POSSESSIVE	families'	students'

- To make a plural noun that does not end in -*s* possessive,
  add an apostrophe and -*s*.

PLURAL	children	deer
PLURAL POSSESSIVE	children's	deer's

PRACTICE

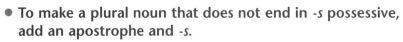

A *Write each phrase using a possessive noun. The first one is done for you.*

1. the work shoes owned by Robert   Robert's work shoes

2. the houses of the neighbors   _____

3. the efforts of the community   _____

4. the vines of the tomatoes   _____

5. the colors of the irises   _____

6. the broccoli belonging to Russ   _____

7. the shovels of the men   _____

8. the nozzles of the hoses   _____

9. the gardens of Miami   _____

10. the work of the people   _____

B *Write the possessive form of the noun in parentheses to correctly complete each sentence.*

1. The _____ office let us use this land for the garden. (mayor)

2. This _____ benefits are obvious to everyone. (garden)

3. The _____ bright colors add beauty to the neighborhood. (flowers)

4. Look at the _____ beautiful flowers. (women)

5. Can you smell the _____ sweet scent? (roses)

6. The _____ bright color shows how fresh the vegetables are. (beans)

7. This _____ size has doubled since yesterday! (zucchini)

8. You can't buy snow peas in the _____ vegetable section. (store)

9. The garden is our _____ favorite meeting place. (community)

10. We find out what is on our _____ minds. (neighbors)

11. My _____ new friend has a garden nearby. (mother)

12. They have a special _____ garden. (children)

C When Sam wrote about his garden, he made six mistakes when writing possessive nouns. Use the proofreading marks in the box to correct all of Sam's errors.

Remember 💡

If a plural noun ends in -s, add only an apostrophe to form the plural possessive. If a plural noun does not end in -s, add 's to form the plural possessive.

Last spring, our family had its first garden. Aprils' warm days had finally arrived. I bought a package of radish seeds and was getting ready to plant them.

"Don't plant them too deep," Dads' voice warned.

I raked the gardens' soil until it was smooth. Then I tore open the packages top and planted a row of seeds. Booker, Mr. Carter's puppy, was watching me. Before I knew it, Booker had grabbed the package and dashed across our garden. By the time I got the package out of Bookers' mouth, he had shaken out the radish seeds— here, there, and everywhere!

"Oh, well, at least you planted one row," Dad said.

Not one seed sprouted in my row of radishes, but all of Booker's seeds sprouted. Thanks to a puppy, our kitchens' refrigerator was full of radishes!

Proofreading Marks

∧	Add
⊙	Period
ℒ	Take out
≡	Capital letter
/	Small letter

Did you correct six possessive nouns?

WRITE

D Write five sentences about a vegetable garden. Use some of the nouns in the box, or use nouns of your own. Include a possessive noun in each sentence.

| blossoms | deer | fall | fence | flowers |
| peas | tomatoes | tool | vegetable | vines |

1. _____

2. _____

3. _____

4. _____

5. _____

Now write five sentences about a park or other outdoor space. Use some of the nouns in the box, or use nouns of your own. Again, include a possessive noun in each sentence.

| child | city | garden | leaves | plants |
| seeds | shovels | soil | trees | weeds |

6. _____

7. _____

8. _____

9. _____

10. _____

Proofreading Checklist ✓

❑ *Did you include a possessive noun in each sentence?*
❑ *Did you spell each possessive noun correctly?*

Lesson 14: Appositives

LEARN

- An **appositive** is a word or phrase that identifies or explains a noun. Appositives follow the nouns they identify or explain.

    Peanut butter, **a popular food**, was invented in 1890. It was called nut paste by its inventor, **a doctor**.

In the sentences above, *a popular food* identifies *peanut butter*. The words *a doctor* identify *inventor*.

- Appositives can make your writing sound better. You can use an appositive to combine two choppy sentences that tell about the same noun.

    Choppy Sentences
    George Bayle was a St. Louis merchant.
    George Bayle sold the first peanut butter.

    Combined with an Appositive
    George Bayle, **a St. Louis merchant**, sold the first peanut butter.

Notice that commas set off the appositive from the rest of the sentence.

Peanut plant

PRACTICE

A *The appositive in each sentence is in **boldface**. Write the noun that the appositive identifies or explains. The first one is done for you.*

1. Peanut butter, **a source of protein**, was an early health food.

_____Peanut butter_____

2. Special tools, **nut grinders**, were used for homemade peanut butter.

_____

3. Roasting, **a processing method**, made the peanuts tasty.

_____

4. George Washington Carver, **an Alabama scientist**, found 300 uses for peanuts.

_____

5. Peanut production, **once a small industry**, grew in importance.

_____

6. A famous peanut farmer is Jimmy Carter, **America's 39th president**. _____

7. Early customers disliked peanut butters' grittiness, **a quality of the product**. _____

8. Churning, **a processing method**, made peanut butter creamy. _____

9. Another variety, **chunky**, is also popular. _____

10. Peanut butter, **a food in most homes**, is here to stay! _____

B *In each sentence, underline all the words in the appositive. The first one is done for you.*

1. A favorite sandwich, the submarine, has a colorful history.

2. Italian immigrants baked *muffoletta*, a special type of bread.

3. Sometimes they filled the bread with ricotta and salami, types of cheese and meat.

4. The sandwich, a meal in itself, was popular with workers.

5. Americans soon added other ingredients, turkey or roast beef.

6. How did these sandwiches, submarines, get their unusual name?

7. In the 1940s, a Connecticut deli delivered hundreds of the sandwiches every day to the same address, a nearby submarine base.

8. Submarine builders, workers at the base, called them subs.

9. One writer, Clementine Paddleford, said only a hero could eat one of the huge sandwiches.

10. The sandwich soon had another name, the hero.

11. Another variety, the six-foot sub, is popular at parties.

12. The bread, a long roll, is one thing the sandwiches have in common.

C *Write an appositive to complete each sentence. Choose an appositive from the box, or use an appositive of your own.*

Remember
Use commas to set off an appositive in a sentence.

> the large size   mushrooms and green peppers   Anthony's
>
> anchovies   a popular food item   a rectangle

1. My favorite pizza toppings, _____, add flavor.

2. My brother Alan dislikes only one topping, _____.

3. A pizza pie, _____, is usually cut into eight slices.

4. Another shape, _____, is usually cut into more slices.

5. Our favorite pizzeria, _____, makes delicious pizza.

6. Frozen pizza, _____, is available in grocery stores.

> a city in southern Italy   a spicy herb   an import from Italy
>
> a fruit new to Europe   a huge quantity   a soft white cheese

7. Pizza, _____, is America's favorite food.

8. Twenty-three pounds, _____, is the amount of pizza the average American eats in a year.

9. Modern pizza was first made in Naples, _____.

10. The cooks of Naples were among the first to use tomatoes,

_____.

11. Early pizza makers used a great deal of basil, _____.

12. Mozzarella, _____, was first added to pizza in 1889.

WRITE

D *Combine each pair of sentences by using an appositive. Write the new sentence on the line. Remember to use commas to set off the appositive. The first one is done for you.*

1. Corn was grown in Mexico more than 5000 years ago.
Corn is an ancient crop.

 Corn, an ancient crop, was grown in Mexico more than 5000 years ago.

2. Hernán Cortés was a Spanish explorer.
Hernán Cortés described tortillas in 1520.

_____

3. Tacos are tortillas wrapped around a filling.
Tacos are a delicious food.

_____

4. Leo is an excellent cook.
Leo makes tacos for his friends and family.

_____

5. *Taco al pastor* is a special kind of taco.
Taco al pastor is made with thinly sliced pork.

_____

6. Ensenada is the birthplace of the fish taco.
Ensenada is a coastal city in Mexico.

_____

7. Burritos are sometimes called breakfast tacos.
Burritos are Rachel's favorite food.

_____

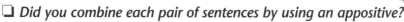

Proofreading Checklist ✔

❑ *Did you combine each pair of sentences by using an appositive?*
❑ *Did you use commas to separate the appositive from the rest of the sentence?*

Unit 2 Review
Lessons 10–14

Common and Proper Nouns (pp. 48–51) *Find the proper noun in each sentence. Capitalize the proper noun, and write it correctly on the line.*

1. You can visit a living history museum in williamsburg. _____

2. This beautiful city became the capital of virginia in 1699. _____

3. For a while, george washington had his headquarters there. _____

4. He prepared for the fight that is now known as the battle of yorktown. _____

5. One building, the governor's palace, is especially grand. _____

6. In 1780, the capital was moved to Richmond. _____

Singular and Plural Nouns (pp. 52–55) *Read each sentence. Write the plural form of the noun in parentheses to complete the sentence.*

7. Williamsburg was once the finest city in the (colony). _____

8. The city was known for its beautiful (church) and parks. _____

9. Williamsburg's streets had numerous small (business). _____

10. Jewelers built (watch) and clocks. _____

11. Potters and silversmiths made fine (dish) and silverware. _____

12. Skilled craftspeople built barrels, (box), and furniture. _____

Irregular Plural Nouns (pp. 56–59) *Read each sentence. Write the plural form of the noun in parentheses to complete the sentence.*

13. During the American Revolution, the sound of soldiers' (foot) rang through Williamsburg.

_____

14. Many great American (hero) lived there.

_____

15. They risked their (life) and fortunes in the struggle for liberty.

_____

16. The (roof) of the old buildings sagged and collapsed.

_____

17. Cows and (sheep) grazed along the streets.

_____

Possessive Nouns (pp. 60–63) *Read each sentence. Write the possessive form of the noun in parentheses to complete the sentence.*

18. (William Goodwin) idea was to rebuild the city as a museum.

_____

19. Restoring Williamsburg became his (life) goal.

_____

20. In the 1920s, Goodwin received a wealthy (man) help.

_____

21. John D. Rockefeller, Jr., bought the (city) oldest buildings.

_____

22. The museum had the local (residents) support.

_____

Appositives (pp. 64–67) *In each sentence, underline all of the words in the appositive. Then circle the noun the appositive identifies or explains.*

23. Williamsburg, the country's oldest living museum, is full of history.

24. Many tourists, Americans and foreigners, visit every year.

25. Friendly hosts, townspeople in colonial dress, welcome the visitors.

26. Colonial life, an important part of our history, has been saved forever.

DIRECTIONS *Fill in the circle next to the sentence that shows correct spelling and the correct use of capital letters and punctuation.*

1. ○ Hawaii is made up of 132 islands in the pacific ocean.
   ○ Hawaii is the only state not on the mainland of North America.
   ○ Honolulu is the largest City.
   ○ Hawaii is also the American State farthest south.

2. ○ Hawaii the youngest state, joined the United States in 1959.
   ○ It was once our countrys territory.
   ○ This state's beauty is famous.
   ○ Hawaii has deep blue seas, white beachs, and brilliant flowers.

3. ○ Hawaii is a Chain of islands.
   ○ It is in the middle of the Pacific, the world's largest ocean.
   ○ All the islands are the tips of huge Volcanoes.
   ○ Mauna Loa, an active volcano is one of earth's largest mountains.

4. ○ Hawaii is the largest Island.
   ○ The island called Maui is known for its mountains.
   ○ A third island, Molokai, has many cattle ranchs.
   ○ Oahu is home to 80 percent of the states people.

5. ○ This states' climate is perfect.
   ○ Winds and Ocean Currents keep the temperature mild.
   ○ Some parts of Hawaii get over 300 inchs of rain a year.
   ○ Water temperatures at Waikiki Beach are always warm.

6. ○ Rich soil is one of Hawaiis resources.
   ○ Farmers grow sugar cane, floweres, and pineapples.
   ○ Steep Mountains limit farming.
   ○ Growing cities replace farmland.

7. ○ Tourism is the most important Industry.
   ○ The state is many peoples first choice for vacation.
   ○ The busiest Months are July, August, and December.
   ○ The beauty of the islands meets most tourists' expectations.

8. ○ People who fly to Hawaii have to reset their watches.
   ○ Hawaii has its own Time zone, the Hawaiian Time Zone.
   ○ When it is 5 o'clock in the evening in boston, it is noon in Hawaii.
   ○ The time in Boston is 5 hours later than in oahu.

DIRECTIONS *Read the paragraphs, and look carefully at each underlined*
part. Fill in the circle next to the answer choice that shows correct spelling
and the correct use of capital letters and punctuation. If the underlined
part is already correct, fill in the circle for "Correct as is."

The first Hawaiians arrived 1500 years ago. These brave settlers sailed

from asia in boats called catamarans. No one knows how they found Hawaii,
         (9)   (10)
a tiny dot in the vast Pacific ocean. The travelers must have carried supplys to
         (10)   (11)
start their colonys. On the Islands, the people's way of life changed, and they
    (11)   (12)
became farmers.

James Cook, an Englishman, and his men reached Hawaii in January of
      (13)
1778. Cook named the many islands the Sandwich Islands. Hawaiians were

eager to trade for the Englishmens iron axs and knifes. In 1820, American
                        (14)
missionaries became the islands' first immigrants.

9. ○ Asia in boats called catamarans
   ○ asia in Boats called catamarans
   ○ Asia, in boats called catamarans
   ○ Correct as is

10. ○ Hawaii a tiny dot in the vast
      Pacific Ocean
   ○ Hawaii, a tiny dot, in the vast
      pacific Ocean
   ○ Hawaii, a tiny dot in the vast
      Pacific Ocean
   ○ Correct as is

11. ○ supplys to start their colonies
   ○ supplies' to start their colony's
   ○ supplies to start their colonies
   ○ Correct as is

12. ○ the islands, the peoples'
   ○ the Islands, the peoples
   ○ the islands, the people's
   ○ Correct as is

13. ○ James cook, an Englishman,
   ○ James Cook an Englishman
   ○ James Cook an Englishman,
   ○ Correct as is

14. ○ Englishmens' iron axes and knives
   ○ Englishmen's iron axs and knifes
   ○ Englishmen's iron axes and knives
   ○ Correct as is

Lesson 15: **Action Verbs**

LEARN

■ The verb is the main word in the predicate. Most verbs are action verbs. An **action verb** tells what the subject *does* or *did*.

> Beth often **rides** a horse.
> At her command, the horse **trotted** up the hill.

■ Action verbs also tell about actions you cannot see.

> Beth **knows** many facts about horses.
> She always **loved** horses.

PRACTICE

A *The predicate is in **boldface**. Write the action verb in the predicate.*

1. Beth **visited the Davis Stables on Thursday**. _____

2. A few horses **stood in the stalls**. _____

3. Beth **enjoyed her riding lesson**. _____

4. Mrs. Davis **saddles Ranger for a ride**. _____

5. The white mare **whinnies at Beth**. _____

6. Beth **remembers last week's lesson**. _____

7. She **balances herself in the saddle carefully**. _____

8. Her hands **hold the reins loosely**. _____

9. Mrs. Davis and Beth **walk their horses at first**. _____

10. Then the horses **gallop down the trail**. _____

B *Draw a line between the subject and the predicate of each sentence. Then write the action verb. The first one is done for you.*

1. The Davis Stables|sponsors a horse show every year.   **sponsors**

2. Many people show their horses there.   _____

3. The show lasts all weekend.   _____

4. Large horse trailers fill the parking lot.   _____

5. Every exhibitor grooms his or her horse carefully.   _____

6. A large crowd gathers in the stands every morning.   _____

7. A lively parade opens each day's show.   _____

8. The riders wave to the crowd.   _____

9. Their colorful Western outfits flash in the sun.   _____

10. The judges examined each horse's movements.   _____

11. They watched each horse and rider carefully.   _____

12. The horses performed many tests at the show.   _____

13. In one event, horses moved through an obstacle course.   _____

14. In another event, horses stepped quickly in exact patterns.   _____

15. The best-trained horses received ribbons and medals.   _____

C *Write an action verb to complete each sentence. Choose a verb from the box, or use a verb of your own.*

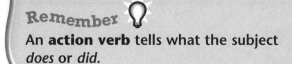

Remember

An **action verb** tells what the subject *does* or *did*.

achieve	choose	compete	cross	live
make	protect	pull	respond	ride
roam	run	scramble	vary	weigh

1. Horses _____ greatly in size, strength, and speed.

2. Ponies _____ great pets for children.

3. Many ponies _____ 40 years or longer.

4. Powerful draft horses _____ heavy wagons and loads.

5. These workhorses _____ a ton or more.

6. Working cowhands usually _____ quarterhorses.

7. These sure-footed horses _____ up steep hillsides.

8. Quarterhorses _____ swift streams without difficulty.

9. They _____ quickly to a rider's commands.

10. Thoroughbred horses _____ in horse races.

11. They _____ faster and longer than other breeds of horses.

12. Some thoroughbreds _____ great success and fame.

13. Wild mustangs still _____ freely in parts of the American West.

14. Federal laws _____ these wild horses.

15. Horse lovers _____ among many different types of horses.

WRITE

D Write three or more sentences about each picture. Use verbs that tell about the action in each picture.

_____

_____

_____

_____

_____

_____

_____

_____

Proofreading Checklist ☑

❏ _Did you use an action verb in each sentence?_
❏ _Did you capitalize and punctuate each sentence correctly?_

Lesson 16: **Direct Objects**

LEARN

A **direct object** is a noun or pronoun that receives the action of the verb. It appears in the predicate part of a sentence.

A direct object answers the question *what* or *whom* after an action verb.

> A freak blizzard hit **Greenville**.
> A freak blizzard hit *what?* (Greenville)

> Our neighborhood lost its **power**.
> Our neighborhood lost *what?* (power)

> The snowstorm surprised **us** overnight.
> The snowstorm surprised *whom?* (us)

> The blackout worried our anxious **neighbors**.
> The blackout worried *whom?* (neighbors)

PRACTICE

A *In each sentence, draw one line under the verb. Draw two lines under the direct object. The first one is done for you.*

1. Thick ice and snow <u>covered</u> the <u><u>trees</u></u>.

2. The strong winds broke many branches.

3. The falling branches tore some wires.

4. The blackout scared my little brother.

5. My parents comforted him.

6. Dad lit some candles in the living room.

7. Mom reported the power outage.

8. The electric company received many calls.

9. Several of my friends called me.

10. Their houses lost power, too.

B *Draw one line under the verb. Draw two lines under the direct object.*
*If there is no direct object, write **no direct object**.*

1. Mom lit a fire in the fireplace.   _____

2. Soon a fire burned brightly.   _____

3. Dad started the grill outside.   _____

4. He barbecued our dinner there.   _____

5. We invited our next-door neighbors to the barbecue.   _____

6. Everyone complimented Dad on his cooking.   _____

7. The whole neighborhood was dark.   _____

8. Then some of my friends arrived.   _____

9. Mom invited them inside.   _____

10. Dad told some funny stories.   _____

11. My friends and I played a game.   _____

12. Then we all sang together.   _____

13. We made popcorn in the fireplace.   _____

14. Nobody missed the TV.   _____

15. We forgot the blackout for a while.   _____

Write a direct object to complete each sentence. Choose a direct object from the box, or use a direct object of your own.

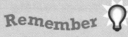

Remember
A direct object receives the action of the verb. It answers the question *what* or *whom.*

cereal	driveway	electricity	friend	lights
Mrs. O'Keefe	power	sidewalks	sleds	snow fort
snowman	streets	television	us	wires

1. In the morning, our neighborhood still had no _____.

2. Deep snow blocked the _____.

3. Mom woke _____ very early.

4. For breakfast, we ate cold _____.

5. Then Dad and I shoveled the _____.

6. I called my best _____.

7. Giant city snowplows cleared the _____.

8. Power company workers repaired the _____.

9. My friends and I built a huge _____ on our lawn.

10. We also made a smiling _____.

11. Maya and I helped _____ for a while.

12. Then we took our _____ to the park.

13. Walking home, we saw _____ in people's houses.

14. We also heard a loud _____.

15. Our neighborhood had _____ once again!

WRITE

D *Imagine that there is a power blackout in your neighborhood. Write five sentences that tell what you and your family do. Use an action verb and a direct object in each sentence. Underline each action verb once and each direct object twice.*

_____

_____

_____

_____

_____

_____

Now write five sentences that tell how to prepare for a blackout or other emergency. Again, use an action verb and direct object in each sentence. Underline each action verb once and each direct object twice.

_____

_____

_____

_____

_____

_____

Proofreading Checklist ✔

❑ *Does each sentence contain an action verb?*
❑ *Does each sentence contain a direct object?*

Lesson 17: **Present-Tense Verbs**

LEARN

■ The **tense** of a verb tells when an action happens. A verb in the **present tense** tells about an action that is happening now.

> Gary **visits** the apes at the zoo.

■ A verb must *agree* with its subject. If the subject is singular or *he, she,* or *it,* the verb must be singular. If the subject is plural or *I, we, you,* or *they,* the verb must be plural.

> Gary **finds** information about gorillas.
> He **writes** a good report.
>
> The girls **like** chimpanzees.
> They **write** a report about chimps.

Gorillas

■ Follow these rules for forming present-tense verbs.

- **Add -s to form most present-tense singular verbs.**
  Sarah read**s** a book about chimps.

- **Add -es if the verb ends in s, ch, sh, x, or z.**
  She watch**es** these apes at the zoo, too.

- **If the verb ends in a consonant and y, change the y to i and add -es.**
  A chimp hurr**ies** from tree to tree.

- **Do not add -s or -es to form a plural verb in the present tense.**
  Chimps **eat** mostly fruit.   I often **watch** the chimps.

PRACTICE

A *Choose the verb in parentheses that agrees with the subject. Then write the verb on the line.*

1. A male gorilla _____ about 400 pounds. (weigh, weighs)

2. The females _____ much less. (weigh, weighs)

3. Chimpanzees _____ in bands. (travel, travels)

4. Each band _____ in size. (vary, varies)

5. An orangutan often _____ alone. (live, lives)

6. It _____ for fruit to eat. (search, searches)

7. I _____ the differences between apes and monkeys. (know, knows)

8. For one thing, apes _____ tails. (lack, lacks)

9. An ape also _____ more intelligence than a monkey. (possess, possesses)

10. You _____ an ape's intelligence all the time. (notice, notices)

B *Write the present-tense form of the verb in parentheses that correctly completes each sentence.*

1. At sunset, the gorilla band _____ to a nesting site. (rush)

2. A mother _____ a nest-and-a-half for herself and her baby. (construct)

3. Usually, night _____ quietly for the gorilla band. (pass)

4. The adult male gorilla _____ the band. (guard)

5. He _____ to protect it from danger. (try)

6. The adult male _____ in alarm at the first sight of people. (cry)

7. He also _____ his fists in anger. (clench)

8. At daylight, the gorilla band _____ into the jungle. (scurry)

9. The endless search for food _____ again. (begin)

C *In these paragraphs from a report about chimpanzees, Ivana has made nine errors in subject-verb agreement. Use the proofreading marks to correct the errors.*

Remember
A verb must *agree* with its subject. If the subject is singular, the verb must be singular. If the subject is plural, the verb must be plural.

The scientist Jane Goodall study chimps in Tanzania and writes about their use of tools. The right tool makes a job easier. Chimpanzees knows that. For example, chimps often "fish" for termites. They pushes a stick into a termite mound. Tasty insects attaches themselves to the stick. Then the chimp pulls the stick out and eats the tasty bugs.

Jane Goodall says chimps use sticks in other ways, too. They comb themselves with twigs. They reaches hard-to-get objects with long branches. Sometimes chimps carries their favorite sticks with them, too.

Other scientists watches chimps using cameras. Sometimes a camera spy a chimp with a tool. On one videotape, a mother chimp teach her babies to crack hard nuts with a rock.

Proofreading Marks

∧	Add
⊙	Period
ℓ	Take out
≡	Capital letter
/	Small letter

Did you find and correct nine errors in subject-verb agreement?

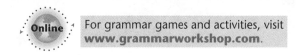

WRITE

Sometimes you may write two sentences that refer to the same subject.

> Orangutans grasp branches with their hands and feet.
> They swing through the trees.

You can make your writing smoother by combining these sentences. The combined sentence will have one subject and a compound predicate.

> Orangutans grasp branches with their hands and feet
> **and** swing through the trees.

Notice that the complete predicates of the two sentences have been combined with the word *and***.**

D *Combine each pair of sentences by writing a sentence with a compound predicate. Write the new sentence on the line.*

1. Male orangutans grow up to $4\frac{1}{2}$ feet tall. They weigh up to 200 pounds.

_____

2. These shy apes usually live alone. These shy apes spend their days searching for food.

_____

3. A male orangutan's call travels long distances. This call protects his large territory.

_____

4. Females and their offspring live together about seven years. They share the same nests.

_____

5. Orangutans search for fruit with sticks. Orangutans use leaves for umbrellas.

_____

6. Orangutans live for about 40 years in the wild. They survive much longer in captivity.

_____

Lesson 18: **Past-Tense Verbs**

LEARN

■ A **past-tense** verb tells about an action that already happened.

> The students **presented** a play.
> Even George **remembered** his lines.

■ Follow these rules for forming past-tense verbs.
- **Add *-ed* to most verbs.**

> Our class **performed** *Peter Pan*.
> I **worked** backstage.

- **If a verb ends in *e*, drop the *e* and add *-ed*.**

> The audience **loved** the sets.

- **If a verb ends in a consonant and *y*, change the *y* to *i* and add *-ed*.**

> We **worried** about the lights.

- **For most one-syllable verbs that end in one vowel followed by one consonant, double the consonant and add *-ed*.**

> Our school **planned** a huge cast party.

PRACTICE

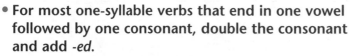 *Write the past-tense form of each verb.*

1. carry _____

2. laugh _____

3. move _____

4. drag _____

5. plot _____

6. wrap _____

7. dry _____

8. receive _____

9. guide _____

10. bury _____

B *Write the past-tense form of the verb in parentheses that correctly completes each sentence.*

1. Mrs. Crandall _____ the script. (prepare)

2. She _____ the play by J. M. Barrie. (adapt)

3. All the fifth graders _____ with the play. (help)

4. I _____ for the role of Captain Hook. (audition)

5. Roger _____ the part of Peter Pan really well. (act)

6. The actors _____ their parts. (memorize)

7. Many parents _____ their time to the play. (contribute)

8. Mrs. Davis _____ the great costumes. (create)

9. Mr. Huang _____ all the scenery. (design)

10. He _____ to finish the sets by opening night. (hurry)

11. The audience members _____ in the action. (participate)

12. They _____ hard for Tinker Bell. (applaud)

13. The applause _____ the show five times! (stop)

14. The fierce-looking pirates _____ the children in the audience. (frighten)

15. The show's success really _____ me! (surprise)

HILLCREST ELEMENTARY SCHOOL presents
Peter Pan
february 9-10

C *Denise wrote these diary entries about her role in the play* **Peter Pan**. *She made ten mistakes when spelling past-tense verbs. Read the entries and find the mistakes. Use the proofreading marks in the box to correct the errors.*

January 12

I am so disappointed. Mrs. Crandall picked Meghan to be Tinker Bell. After hearing the news, Meghan danced beautifully across the stage. She flaped her arms like Tinker Bell's wings. I almost cryed.

Mrs. Crandall asked me to be Meghan's backup. I replyed, "Okay." I smileed, but inside, my spirits droped. I guess I tryed out for the wrong part!

January 30

Meghan broke her leg, and I'm playing Tinker Bell! I studyed my lines for hours. At my first rehearsal, I missd many lines. Then I triped over some scenery. I hopped I'd be a star, but it didn't turn out that way.

Proofreading Marks

∧	Add
⊙	Period
ℒ	Take out
≡	Capital letter
/	Small letter

Did you fix the spelling of ten past-tense verbs?

WRITE

D *Write about a play that you have seen. Write an answer for each item below about the play. In each answer, use the past tense of the verb in parentheses. The first one is done for you.*

1. Tell the name of the play you saw. (attend) _____

  Last year, I attended a musical performance of *Cinderella*. _____

2. Tell what you enjoyed most about the play. (like) _____

_____

3. Tell when and where the show took place. (open) _____

_____

4. Tell how the stagehands set up your favorite scene. (prepare) _____

_____

5. Tell about an actor who made a mistake. (hesitate) _____

_____

6. Tell how you know the audience liked the play. (clap) _____

_____

7. Tell who got the most applause and why. (receive) _____

_____

8. Tell something the play taught you. (learn) _____

_____

Proofreading Checklist ✓

❑ *Did you use the verb in parentheses in each sentence?*
❑ *Did you spell each past-tense verb correctly?*

Lesson 19: **Future-Tense Verbs**

LEARN

■ Present-tense verbs tell about actions that happen now. Past-tense verbs tell about actions that already happened. **Future-tense** verbs tell about actions that are going to happen.

PRESENT	The U.S. Congress **passes** our nation's laws.
PAST	Congress **passed** a law yesterday.
FUTURE	Congress **will pass** other laws next week.

■ Use the verb *will* with the main verb to form the future tense. *Shall* is sometimes used when the subject is *I* or *we*.

I **shall write** to my congresswoman soon.
We **will see** our lawmakers at work.

PRACTICE

A *Write present, past, or future to tell the tense of the verb in boldface.*

1. We **visited** the U.S. Congress recently. _____

2. Members of Congress **discuss** many issues. _____

3. We **observed** the House of Representatives last Tuesday. _____

4. The representatives **debated** four bills yesterday. _____

5. These bills **will become** laws later this month. _____

6. The voters **will elect** members of Congress next November. _____

7. We **shall work** in our congresswoman's campaign. _____

8. We **visit** the Senate right now. _____

9. Our senator **delivered** a speech there earlier. _____

10. You **will read** about it in the newspaper tomorrow. _____

B *Write the correct tense of the verb in parentheses to complete each sentence.*

1. Last week, we _____ the three branches of government. (study)

2. Members of Congress _____ our nation's laws. (make)

3. Congress _____ a bill last month. (pass)

4. Now the bill _____ on the president's desk. (sit)

5. Next Monday, the president _____ it into law. (sign)

6. I _____ that bill-signing ceremony on TV next week. (watch)

7. Last year, the president _____ some of the bills passed by Congress. (reject)

8. As head of the executive branch, the president _____ the laws. (enforce)

9. We _____ the Supreme Court tomorrow. (visit)

10. Yesterday, the Supreme Court _____ a law unconstitutional. (declare)

11. Tomorrow morning, attorneys _____ another case before the Supreme Court. (argue)

12. The nine Supreme Court judges _____ that case later this year. (decide)

13. The three branches of government _____ our country well. (serve)

14. You _____ more about these three branches in years to come. (learn)

15. I _____ as soon as I turn 18. (vote)

C *Annie is writing a letter to her state senator. In her first draft, she made eight mistakes with present-, past-, and future-tense verbs. Use the proofreading marks in the box to correct all of the mistakes.*

Remember
Use the verb *will* or *shall* with the main verb to form the future tense. The verb *shall* is only used when the subject is *I* or *we*.

Dear Senator Gutierrez:

Last year, the Senate pass the State Wildlife Grants Program. This program helps wildlife from becoming endangered. More bald eagles now nested in our state than ever before!

Yesterday, I notice a report in the <u>Daily Post</u>. You will decide last week to vote against funding the program. I hope you will reconsider.

Without this program, the wilderness in our state disappear. Animals will lose their habitats, and our citizens lose their natural heritage.

Your "yes" vote make a difference. Please vote "yes," and we support you next Election Day!

Sincerely,

Annie Davies

Proofreading Marks

∧	Add
⊙	Period
⌿	Take out
≡	Capital letter
/	Small letter

Did you correct eight verbs that were in the wrong tense?

Online · For grammar games and activities, visit
www.grammarworkshop.com.

WRITE

D *Read each item. Some of the verbs in the sentences
are in the wrong tense. Rewrite each item so that all
of the verbs are in the correct tense.*

VOTE FOR HAL GREEN

1. Senator Hal Green will travel to Johnson Falls next Friday
at 4:00 P.M. He give a speech at our new town library. Many
people gathered there. They will thank the senator for his
support of the library.

_____

_____

_____

2. On Election Day next Tuesday, the polls opened at 6:00 A.M. Senator
Green's name be on the ballot, and many people vote for him.

_____

_____

3. My parents moved to Johnson Falls last year. They register to vote right
away. They vote for Senator Green tomorrow on Election Day. Probably,
he win another term in office.

_____

_____

_____

4. We watch the election returns on TV tomorrow night. The news anchor
discusses the election. He announced the vote counts, too. Will Senator
Green win? We know tomorrow night!

_____

_____

_____

Lesson 20: Linking Verbs

LEARN

- A linking verb does not show action. A **linking verb** links the subject of a sentence to a noun or an adjective in the predicate.

  The noun that follows the linking verb names the subject.

  Rocky Point **is** a beach.

  The adjective that follows a linking verb describes the subject.

  This beach **is** always so beautiful!

- Linking verbs are often forms of the verb *be*: *am, is, are, was, were,* and *will be*. The verbs *look, seem, appear, taste, sound, smell, feel,* and *become* are also common linking verbs.

  Those white birds **are** seagulls.

  The air at the beach **smells** salty today.

  The water in the pool **feels** very warm.

PRACTICE

A *Write the linking verb in each sentence.*

1. The tide is low now. _____

2. It will be higher later. _____

3. Those shellfish are mussels. _____

4. They taste delicious! _____

5. The gulls sound noisy today. _____

6. The beach was empty yesterday. _____

7. This little creature is a jellyfish. _____

8. It appears harmless. _____

9. Those marks in the sand are my footprints. _____

10. The wet sand feels good under our feet. _____

B *Read each sentence. Write the linking verb and the noun or adjective that the verb links to the subject. The first one is done for you.*

1. The seashore becomes rocky over here. ____becomes   rocky____

2. These big puddles are tidal pools. _____

3. Each tidal pool is a little world of plants and animals. _____

4. I am curious about sea creatures. _____

5. Those seashells were once the homes of sea animals. _____

6. Seaweed is a plant without roots. _____

7. Old seaweed on the beach sometimes smells bad. _____

8. In the water, the seaweed appears beautiful. _____

9. These sea sponges feel soft to the touch. _____

10. That crab looks lost. _____

11. These shellfish taste delicious, too. _____

12. This beach seems perfect to me. _____

C *Write a linking verb to complete each sentence. Choose a linking verb from the box.*

 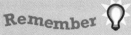
am	appears	are	becomes	feel
feels	is	look	seem	smells
sound	tastes	was	were	will be

1. This sand _____ hot around my ankles.

2. The waves suddenly _____ louder.

3. The tide _____ higher, too.

4. These giant conch shells _____ so beautiful.

5. Perhaps the abandoned shells _____ hiding places for other sea creatures.

6. Those pebbles _____ smooth to the touch.

7. This fossil _____ once a sea animal.

8. I _____ a collector of fossils.

9. The seagulls overhead _____ hungry all the time.

10. Anything _____ good to them.

11. In the bright sunshine, the ocean water _____ green.

12. The salty air _____ so refreshing!

13. The wind _____ gusty by late afternoon.

14. Tomorrow _____ another great day at Rocky Point.

15. The ocean's riches _____ always amazing!

WRITE

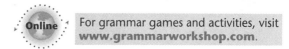
D Write about the picnic scene in the picture. Describe the setting, and tell how the people and food look. Describe how the food tastes, too. Use linking verbs in your sentences.

_____

_____

_____

_____

_____

_____

_____

_____

_____

_____

_____

Proofreading Checklist ☑

❏ _Does each sentence contain a linking verb?_
❏ _Does each linking verb connect the subject of the sentence to a noun or an adjective in the predicate?_

Lesson 21: Main Verbs and Helping Verbs

LEARN

■ A verb may be more than one word. The **main verb** shows the action in the sentence. The **helping verb** helps the main verb show an action. Together, the main verb and the helping verb form a **verb phrase**.

> Mrs. Delgado **has planned** a vacation.
> She and her children **are flying** to Puerto Rico.
> They **will visit** a famous rainforest there.

In the verb phrases above, *planned*, *flying*, and *visit* are the main verbs. *Has*, *are*, and *will* are the helping verbs.

■ In the verb phrases below, *can, could,* and *should* are helping verbs. *Drive, fly,* and *walk* are main verbs.

> **can drive**   **could fly**   **should walk**

Other common helping verbs include *am, is, was, were, shall, have,* and *had*.

PRACTICE

A *Write the verb phrase in each sentence. Draw one line under the helping verb and two lines under the main verb.*

1. The Delgados are driving to the airport. _____

2. They should arrive two hours before their flight. _____

3. Many cars were hurrying to the airport, too. _____

4. The Delgados have parked their car in a parking lot. _____

5. A bus has taken them to the main building. _____

6. Crowds of people are hurrying in all directions. _____

7. Mrs. Delgado is checking the luggage. _____

8. She had purchased her tickets online last month. _____

9. The airline clerk is handing her the boarding passes.   _____

10. Everyone will need a boarding pass later at the gate.   _____

B *Find the verb or verb phrase in each sentence, and write it on the line.*
In each verb phrase, underline the helping verb once and the main verb twice.

1. The Delgados are walking to the security checkpoint.   _____

2. Security officers screen everyone at the checkpoint.   _____

3. No one can carry dangerous objects onto an airplane.   _____

4. An X-ray machine was screening all carry-on bags.   _____

5. Everyone will pass through the metal detector.   _____

6. Mrs. Delgado removes her shoes and belt.   _____

7. Ray and Iris Delgado have removed theirs, too.   _____

8. The metal detector beeps at Ray Delgado.   _____

9. He had overlooked some coins in his pocket.   _____

10. The family has passed through the checkpoint.   _____

11. Now the Delgados should proceed to the gate.   _____

12. The passengers board the plane at Gate 15.   _____

C *Write a helping verb to complete each sentence. Choose a helping verb from the box.*

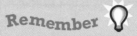

am	are	can	could	had	has
have	is	should	was	were	will

1. The Delgados' plane _____ arriving from another city.

2. At last, the passengers _____ board the plane.

3. Mrs. Delgado _____ handed the boarding passes to a flight attendant.

4. Now the family _____ walking down a ramp and onto the plane.

5. The three Delgados _____ sit in Row 17, Seats A, B, and C.

6. I _____ sitting in the row behind them.

7. Ray and Iris _____ arguing over the window seat.

8. According to Mrs. Delgado, the children _____ take turns in that seat.

9. At first, other passengers _____ placing their bags in the overhead racks.

10. Now they all _____ buckled their seatbelts.

11. Before takeoff, Ray _____ felt a bit nervous.

12. Now he _____ see the ground far below him.

WRITE

Online For grammar games and activities, visit www.grammarworkshop.com.

D *Make up a sentence to answer each question. Include both a helping verb and a main verb in each answer sentence you write. Then underline the verb phrase. The first one is done for you.*

1. Has your family traveled by airplane before?

My family <u>has traveled</u> by airplane before.

2. Is everyone enjoying the flight?

_____

3. At what time should the plane arrive in Puerto Rico?

_____

4. What movie was playing on the airplane?

_____

5. Will you listen to music or sports?

_____

6. Has the flight attendant given you a meal?

_____

7. Are we flying over Florida now?

_____

8. Will the plane land in San Juan, Puerto Rico?

_____

9. How long can your family stay in Puerto Rico?

_____

Proofreading Checklist ✓

❏ *Is each answer a complete sentence?*
❏ *Does each sentence contain a verb phrase?*

Lesson 22: **Using *Be* and *Have***

LEARN

■ The verbs *be* and *have* have special singular and plural forms. Use the forms of *be* and *have* that agree with the subject of the sentence.

Subject	Forms of *be* Present	Past	Forms of *have* Present	Past
Singular nouns *he, she, it*	is	was	has	had
Plural nouns *you, we, they*	are	were	have	had
I	am	was	have	had

Our town's big **race is** today.
Ellen was the winner last year.
We were proud of her.

My dad has a racing trophy.
You have new running shoes.
Our town had one race last year.

■ The verbs *have* and *be* can also be helping verbs. The forms of *have* are used with the past-tense forms (*-ed*) of main verbs. The forms of *be* can be used with main verbs that end in *-ing.* Remember to use the forms of *have* or *be* that agree with the subject of the sentence.

I am training for the race.
My **aunt is running** with me.
We were jogging on the bike path.

Tina has entered the race.
I have finished the race.
We had received our awards.

Remember that when the helping verb *have* is used with the past-tense form of a verb, it shows that an action has already happened.

PRACTICE

A *Write the form of the verb in parentheses that correctly completes each sentence.*

1. I _____ at the school track. (am, is)

2. Dad and I _____ a good run. (has, had)

3. The cool weather _____ perfect for running! (was, were)

4. Running _____ good exercise. (is, are)

5. The 15 Mile Club _____ popular at our school. (is, are)

6. All club members _____ a goal to run 15 miles every week. (has, have)

7. I _____ the idea for this club last year. (has, had)

8. Our school _____ a new track. (has, have)

9. Five-kilometer (5K) races _____ about three miles long. (is, are)

10. We _____ eager for the race to begin. (was, were)

B *Write the helping verb in parentheses that correctly completes each sentence.*

1. Dad _____ jogging with me. (is, are)

2. We _____ just jogged for 30 minutes. (has, have)

3. After that, we _____ feeling great! (was, were)

4. Running _____ helped me get in shape. (has, have)

5. Many fifth grade students _____ discovered running. (has, have)

6. Some students _____ running four times a week. (is, are)

7. We _____ trying to run 15 miles every week. (is, are)

8. Our town _____ sponsoring a five-kilometer (5K) race today. (is, are)

9. I _____ entering the race. (am, is)

10. Last year, our town _____ scheduled a 5K race. (had, have)

11. This year, the committee _____ planned for three races. (has, have)

12. Running _____ becoming more popular every day. (is, are)

C Kathleen wrote the editorial below for the school newspaper. In three sentences, the forms of **be** do not agree with the subject. In five sentences, the helping verbs **has** and **have** do not agree with the subject. Find the mistakes, and use the proofreading marks to correct them.

 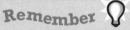
Our new school track is finished! The principal have opened the track officially.

Today I am visiting the track. I has picked a great day. A cool breeze is blowing, and the track's bright green surface am gleaming in the sun.

Two teachers is walking around the track. They has walked one mile already. One classmate am jogging for the very first time. I has changed into my sneakers to join all the joggers.

I don't see many people on the new track. In the past, we had many excuses for not running. The streets were too dangerous for jogging, or the park was too far away. The school's new track have changed all that. Let's get down there and use it!

Proofreading Marks	
∧	Add
⊙	Period
ℒ	Take out
☰	Capital letter
/	Small letter

Did you correct the eight errors in subject-verb agreement?

WRITE

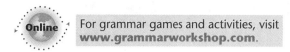
D *Read each part of this story about a race that Vince ran.
Continue each section of the story by writing your own
sentences. Use forms of the verbs **be** and **have** as helping verbs
in your sentences.*

1. Vince is standing at the starting line. He has pinned his number to
his shirt. The other runners are crowding around. Everyone is waiting
for the race to begin. Now the officials

_____

_____

_____

2. Midway through the race, Vince is feeling great. Only a few runners have
passed him. Now Vince has decided to take the lead. He

_____

_____

_____

3. Vince and Tom are running neck and neck. They are closing in on the
finish line. To win the race, Vince

_____

_____

_____

Proofreading Checklist ☑

❏ *Did you write complete sentences to continue each part of
the story?*

❏ *Did you write sentences that contain forms of the verbs **be**
and **have** as helping verbs? Have you used the correct
forms of these two verbs?*

Lesson 23: **Irregular Verbs**

LEARN

■ **Regular verbs** form the past tense by adding *-ed.*
Irregular verbs do not add *-ed* to form the past tense.
Their spellings change in the past tense and in the past
with *has, have,* or *had.*

PRESENT	Tim and May **write** about animal journeys.
PAST	They **wrote** their paper last week.
WITH *HAVE*	The students **have written** a good report.

Irregular Verbs		
Present	**Past**	**Past with Helping Verb**
begin	began	*has, have,* or *had* begun
bring	brought	*has, have,* or *had* brought
choose	chose	*has, have,* or *had* chosen
fly	flew	*has, have,* or *had* flown
go	went	*has, have,* or *had* gone
grow	grew	*has, have,* or *had* grown
make	made	*has, have,* or *had* made
swim	swam	*has, have,* or *had* swum
take	took	*has, have,* or *had* taken
write	wrote	*has, have,* or *had* written

PRACTICE

A *Write the form of the verb in parentheses that correctly completes each sentence.*

1. Autumn _____ on September 21. (began, begun)

2. The days have _____ shorter and the nights longer. (grew, grown)

3. Colder weather has _____ changes to the land. (bring, brought)

4. The animal migrations have _____. (began, begun)

5. The monarch butterflies have _____ to warmer winter homes. (went, gone)

6. Many falcons have _____ south already. (flew, flown)

7. A flock of Canada geese _____ overhead yesterday. (flew, flown)

8. Many whales _____ to warmer waters. (swam, swum)

9. By last Friday, two whales had _____ past our beach. (swam, swum)

10. The seals have _____ their trip south, too. (make, made)

B *Write the past form of the verb in parentheses to correctly complete each sentence.*

1. By September, many animals have _____ their yearly migrations. (begin)

2. They have _____ to warmer places with more food. (go)

3. Last week, the deer _____ a migration down into the valley. (begin)

4. The colder weather has _____ quail and turkeys to the valley, too. (bring)

5. Tim and May have _____ about these migrations in their report. (write)

6. Some gray whales _____ from the Arctic to the waters off the coast of California. (swim)

7. The Arctic tern has _____ over 20,000 miles! (fly)

8. Its migration has _____ it from the North Pole to Antarctica. (take)

9. The woodchucks and chipmunks have _____ heavy coats. (grow)

10. They have only _____ a few feet underground for the winter. (go)

Read this section of Tim and May's report. They made eight mistakes with the past forms of irregular verbs. Use the proofreading marks in the box to correct the errors.

Some animals make one round-trip migration in a lifetime. This Pacific salmon, for example, begun her life in a stream. Once she had grew a few inches, she swam downstream to the ocean. That journey could have taken months.

In the ocean, the salmon ate shrimp and small fish. She growed to full size. After a year or more, the salmon began a difficult trip. She migrated back to the stream where she was born to lay her eggs.

The trip upstream was against the current. The salmon swum hard against rushing water. She jumped up waterfalls. Sometimes, she almost flied through the air! Some salmon have went as far as 2,000 miles upstream!

The long migration had brung the salmon back to her birthplace. The trip, however, had took a lot out of her. After laying her eggs, the salmon died.

Proofreading Marks

∧	Add
⊙	Period
ℓ	Take out
≡	Capital letter
/	Small letter

Pacific salmon

LOOK Back

Did you find and correct eight errors with irregular verbs?

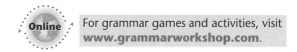

Online   For grammar games and activities, visit
www.grammarworkshop.com.

WRITE

D *Complete the sentences in the paragraphs below with past forms of irregular verbs. Use forms of the verbs in the chart on page 104. Then write a few sentences of your own to complete the last paragraph. Use past forms of irregular verbs in some of your sentences.*

The cold winds of December _____ snow and ice to our area today.

Fortunately, most animals had _____ steps to prepare for the wintry

weather. By late October, most songbirds had _____ south, where food

was plentiful. All the robins _____ away earlier, when the weather was

still fairly warm. This year, for some reason, the Canada geese _____ to

stay around for the winter!

The chipmunks and woodchucks were ready for winter, too. They

_____ their winter sleeps a few weeks ago. During the fall, they

_____ deep holes in the ground to sleep in. They also _____

fat by eating extra food. We won't see them again until spring. The squirrels have

_____ extra nuts up to their nests. So they're ready, too.

Some of our human neighbors have _____ away for the winter, too.

One of our neighbors _____ us a letter from Florida last week.

_____

_____

_____

Proofreading Checklist ☑

❏ *Did you use the correct form of the verb with **has, have**, or **had**?*

❏ *Did you spell the forms of the irregular verbs correctly?*

Lesson 24: **More Irregular Verbs**

LEARN

Irregular verbs do not add *-ed* to form the past tense. Their spellings change to form the past tense and the past with *has, have,* or *had.*

PRESENT	My classmates **speak** about heroes of the American Revolution.
PAST	Our teacher **spoke** about Sybil Ludington.
WITH *HAVE*	We **have spoken** about other female heroes.

Irregular Verbs		
Present	**Past**	**Past with Helping Verb**
break	broke	*has, have,* or *had* broken
blow	blew	*has, have,* or *had* blown
fall	fell	*has, have,* or *had* fallen
know	knew	*has, have,* or *had* known
ride	rode	*has, have,* or *had* ridden
ring	rang	*has, have,* or *had* rung
sing	sang	*has, have,* or *had* sung
speak	spoke	*has, have,* or *had* spoken
throw	threw	*has, have,* or *had* thrown
wear	wore	*has, have,* or *had* worn

PRACTICE

A *Write the form of the verb in parentheses that correctly completes each sentence.*

1. Theo _____ a song about a young American hero. (sang, sung)

2. Until recently, few people have _____ about Sybil Ludington. (knew, known)

3. In 1777, this brave sixteen-year-old _____ through the New York countryside on a dark and rainy night. (ride, rode)

4. A cold wind _____ loudly that April night. (blew, blown)

5. Sybil _____ to local soldiers about a serious event. (speak, spoke)

6. The nearby town of Danbury had just _____ to the British. (fell, fallen)

7. Alarm bells soon _____ in the villages. (rang, rung)

8. Before long, an army of patriots had _____ to Danbury. (rode, ridden)

9. The Patriots _____ through the British lines there. (broke, broken)

10. Thanks to Sybil, the American Patriots _____ the British troops out of Connecticut. (threw, thrown)

B *Write the past form of the verb in parentheses to correctly complete each sentence.*

1. By 1777, many Massachusetts men had _____ to war. (ride)

2. No woman had _____ the American uniform. (wear)

3. In 1778, Deborah Samson _____ that barrier! (break)

4. To sign up, the Massachusetts woman _____ men's clothing. (wear)

5. She had always _____ in a deep voice. (speak)

6. No one in the army _____ her true identity. (know)

7. For three years, Deborah _____ herself into the fighting. (throw)

8. Once she had _____ to the ground with an injury. (fall)

9. Near the end of the war, several officers _____ Samson's secret. (know)

10. She had _____ the rule that kept women out of the army. (break)

11. Nevertheless, General Washington _____ kindly to her. (speak)

12. The brave, young woman _____ home a hero! (ride)

C Allison wrote about another female hero of the American Revolution. In her report, she made nine mistakes using irregular verbs. Use the proofreading marks to correct the errors.

Remember
Irregular verbs do not add *-ed* to form the past tense. They change their spellings instead.

Her real name was Mary Hays, but soldiers known her as "Molly Pitcher."

The date was June 28, 1778. The event was the Battle of Monmouth in New Jersey. Mary had rode there with her husband, William. His job was to fire a cannon.

The temperature was 100 degrees. Hot winds blowed across the battlefield. During the fighting, Mary carried pitcher after pitcher of water to the thirsty soldiers. They all speaked fondly of "Molly Pitcher."

At one point, Molly looked over at her husband. He had fell to the ground. He had broke his leg when a British shell had blowed up near him.

Fortunately, Molly knew how to fire the cannon. She throwed down her pitcher. Instead of carrying water, Molly fired William's cannon for the rest of the battle. She had wore a long skirt that day, but she served as a brave soldier!

Molly helped the Americans win the Battle of Monmouth. Even General Washington spoke highly of her bravery.

Proofreading Marks	
∧	Add
⊙	Period
ℓ	Take out
≡	Capital letter
/	Small letter

Did you find and correct nine errors with irregular verbs?

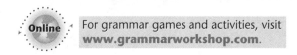

WRITE

D *Complete the sentences in the paragraphs below with past forms of irregular verbs. Use forms of the verbs in the chart on page 108. Then write a few sentences of your own to tell why you think heroes are important. Use past forms of irregular verbs in some of your sentences.*

Many people have _____ about Paul Revere. A famous poem

tells how this hero _____ his horse from Boston to Concord on

April 18, 1775. Revere's warning, "The British are coming!" _____ the

silence of the night. Farmers who had _____ asleep woke up. Thanks to

Revere, they _____ the British soldiers were on the way.

Paul Revere is famous. Until recently, however, few Americans have _____

about William Dawes and Samuel Prescott. No one has _____ songs or

written poems about them. Yet both Dawes and Prescott had _____ their

horses out of Boston with Revere that same April night. Their cries had _____

through the night, too. Without Dawes and Prescott, the American Patriots might

not have _____ that the struggle for freedom had begun!

_____

_____

_____

_____

_____

Proofreading Checklist ✓

❑ *Did you use the correct form of the verb with* **has, have,** *or* **had**?

❑ *Did you spell the forms of the irregular verbs correctly?*

Lesson 25: **Contractions with *Not***

LEARN

A **contraction** is a word formed by joining two words, making one shorter word.

A contraction is often made up of a verb combined with the word *not*. An apostrophe (') takes the place of any letters that are left out.

are + not = **aren't**   do + not = **don't**
The pies **aren't** ready yet.   **Don't** take them out of the oven.

Contractions with *not*			
is not	**isn't**	do not	**don't**
are not	**aren't**	does not	**doesn't**
was not	**wasn't**	did not	**didn't**
were not	**weren't**	cannot	**can't**
will not	**won't**	could not	**couldn't**
has not	**hasn't**	should not	**shouldn't**
have not	**haven't**	would not	**wouldn't**
had not	**hadn't**	must not	**mustn't**

Notice how the contractions for *cannot* and *will not* are formed. In *cannot*, both an *n* and the *o* are dropped. In *will not*, the spelling changes.

can + not = **can't**   will + not = **won't**

PRACTICE

 Write the contraction for each pair of words.

1. had not _____

2. were not _____

3. did not _____

4. could not _____

5. will not _____

6. cannot _____

7. must not _____

8. are not _____

9. does not _____

10. have not _____

B *Read each of the following common expressions. Write a contraction for each pair of words in **boldface**.*

1. It **is not** over till it's over. _____

2. You **have not** seen anything yet. _____

3. We **will not** be undersold! _____

4. There **are not** any easy answers. _____

5. We **could not** see the forest for the trees. _____

6. **Do not** give up the ship! _____

7. That **does not** ring a bell. _____

8. You **must not** say such things! _____

9. **Would not** that be nice! _____

10. I **did not** say a word. _____

11. It **has not** been easy! _____

12. They **were not** so great. _____

13. **Should not** we do something? _____

14. That **was not** my cup of tea. _____

15. You **cannot** get there from here. _____

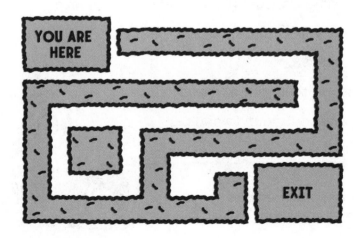

C A group of fifth graders wrote a list of sayings for their friends. They made eight mistakes when they wrote contractions with **not**. Read the sayings. Then use the proofreading marks in the box to correct the mistakes.

- Do'nt trust your dog to watch your snack.
- If you have'nt started your report yet, get going!
- Never put toast on plates that are'nt dry.
- You shouldn't eat a sandwich while riding a bike.
- Drying your jeans with a hairdryer doesn't work very well.
- If you want a puppy, it willn't hurt to show how responsible you are.
- If there wasnt a last minute, some things would never get done.
- If your friend has'nt called you in a while, try giving him or her a call.
- It is'nt a good idea to laugh when you have a mouthful of milk.
- I wouldn't eat a cracker if I was about to sneeze.
- If you cann't get to places on time, start out earlier.
- When someone tells you a secret, you musn't tell all your friends.

Proofreading Marks	
∧	Add
⊙	Period
ℰ	Take out
☰	Capital letter
/	Small letter

Did you correct the mistakes in the eight contractions?

WRITE

Write Your Own

D *Now write some sayings of your own. For each topic below, write one complete sentence that gives a piece of advice. Use a contraction with **not** in each sentence. Your sayings can be funny or serious. The first one is done for you.*

1. Advice About Food

Don't eat snacks with a lot of sugar and fat. _____

_____

2. Advice About Sports

_____

_____

3. Advice About Friends

_____

_____

4. Advice About School

_____

_____

5. Advice About Homework

_____

_____

6. Advice About Pets

_____

_____

Proofreading Checklist ✓

❏ *Did you spell each contraction with **not** correctly?*

Lesson 26: Verbs Often Misused

LEARN

Verbs that have meanings that are related or similar can cause confusion. These include *teach* and *learn*, *sit* and *set*, and *let* and *leave*. Study the meanings of these words so that you use them correctly.

Meaning	Example
teach—to give knowledge	The Smiths **teach** their dogs tricks.
learn—to get knowledge	Some dogs **learn** quickly.
sit—to rest	The dogs **sit** in front of a hoop.
set—to put or place; to establish	The Smiths **set** the hoop on a high stand.
let—to allow or permit	The Smiths **let** me pet their dogs.
leave—to go away from; to let remain in place	The Smiths **leave** for a dog show today. Please **leave** the leash by the door.

PRACTICE

A *Write **teach** or **learn** to correctly complete each sentence.*

1. You can _____ a young dog new tricks.

2. Young dogs _____ faster than old dogs.

3. Most people _____ their dogs to lie down.

4. Many dogs _____ to stay, too.

*Write **sit** or **set** to correctly complete each sentence.*

5. A dog should _____ on command.

6. We _____ aside time for training our dog.

7. Please _____ that dog food down.

*Write **let** or **leave** to correctly complete each sentence.*

8. The dogs _____ the room quietly.

9. Please _____ me walk your dog.

10. My dog will _____ you pet her.

B *Write the word in parentheses that correctly completes each sentence.*

1. At the dog show, many dog lovers _____ in the stands. (sit, set)

2. These fans will _____ many things about dogs tonight. (teach, learn)

3. Please _____ these grooming tools on that table. (leave, let)

4. The judges at the show _____ very high standards. (sit, set)

5. Many dog owners _____ professional trainers handle their dogs. (let, leave)

6. Trainers _____ their dogs to ignore other dogs at the show. (teach, learn)

7. All dogs must _____ the judges examine them. (leave, let)

8. Dogs must also _____ still for long periods of times. (sit, set)

9. Trainers also _____ dogs to walk in figure eights. (teach, learn)

10. Dogs _____ quickly when they are praised often. (teach, learn)

11. The judges _____ different classes of dogs enter the ring. (leave, let)

12. I could _____ in this seat and watch these dogs for days! (sit, set)

13. The losing dogs _____ the show ring gracefully. (let, leave)

14. The judges _____ the trophies on the tables. (sit, set)

15. _____ me take a photo of the dog that was "Best in Show." (Let, Leave)

C *Mr. Smith wrote these rules for training a dog. He made eight mistakes when using the verb pairs **teach** and **learn**, **sit** and **set**, and **let** and **leave**. Use the proofreading marks in the box to correct the mistakes.*

Remember 💡
Learn the meanings of the verb pairs *teach* and *learn*, *sit* and *set*, and *let* and *leave* to use them correctly.

Keep training sessions short. Puppies and dogs have short attention spans. Set a time limit of 10 or 15 minutes for each training session. Usually, you can learn a dog more in 10 minutes than in half an hour. Never leave a dog get bored with its training.

Stay Calm and in Control. Training should be enjoyable for you and your dog. If you can't control your feelings, set down or leave the room.

Reinforce with Praise. When your dog learns a lesson, praise it. If your dog doesn't learn a lesson, never hit it. You cannot learn a dog anything by punishing it.

Be Consistent. In each session, know exactly what you want to learn your dog. Set simple goals. For example, don't leave the dog get confused by trying to learn it too much in one session.

End on a Positive Note. Every training session should end with praise. Provide a treat and words of praise. Otherwise, your dog might set down and not take part in the next session.

Proofreading Marks	
∧	Add
⊙	Period
ℓ	Take out
≡	Capital letter
/	Small letter

Did you correct eight mistakes with the verb pairs *teach* and *learn*, *sit* and *set*, and *let* and *leave*?

WRITE

D *Follow the directions for each numbered item. In your sentences, underline the verbs (**teach**, **learn**; **let**, **leave**; **sit**, **set**) that you have been asked to use.*

1. Write two or three sentences that tell what you would like to teach a dog or other pet to do. Use the verbs *teach* and *learn* in your sentences.

_____

_____

_____

_____

2. Write two or three questions that you might ask the owners of prize-winning dogs. Use the verbs *let* and *leave* in some of your questions.

_____

_____

_____

_____

3. Write two or three sentences that tell why it is important for dog owners to train their dogs to follow commands, such as *sit* and *stay*. Use the verbs *sit* and *set* in your sentences.

_____

_____

_____

_____

Proofreading Checklist ☑

❏ *Did you use the verbs **teach** and **learn** correctly in item 1?*
❏ *Did you use the verbs **leave** and **let** correctly in item 2?*
❏ *Did you use the verbs **set** and **sit** correctly in item 3?*

Action Verbs and Direct Objects (pp. 72–79) *Draw one line under the action verb. Draw two lines under the direct object.*

1. People today need forests.

2. Many animals make their homes in the forest.

3. Trees also prevent floods.

Present-Tense Verbs (pp. 80–83) *Write the present-tense form of the verb in parentheses to correctly complete each sentence.*

4. This forest (stretch) for miles.   _____

5. Its trees (provide) wood for thousands of products.   _____

6. The forest (supply) us with oxygen, too.   _____

Past-Tense Verbs (pp. 84–87) *Write the past-tense form of the verb in parentheses to correctly complete each sentence.*

7. Forests (cover) much of our continent at one time.   _____

8. Early settlers (chop) down many of the forests.   _____

9. Environmentalists (save) many forests last year.   _____

Future-Tense Verbs (pp. 88–91) *Write the correct tense of the verb in parentheses to complete each sentence.*

10. Our class (visit) a nearby forest last week.   _____

11. We (return) for another visit next week.   _____

12. The park rangers (guide) us then.   _____

Linking Verbs (pp. 92–95) *Write the linking verb and the noun or adjective that the verb links to the subject.*

13. The forest seems peaceful.   _____

14. The spruce trees are evergreens.   _____

15. The entire forest smells fragrant.   _____

Main Verbs and Helping Verbs (pp. 96–99) *Draw one line under the helping verb. Draw two lines under the main verb.*

16. People should visit forests more often.

17. You can see so much here.

18. The leaves are rustling in the breeze.

Using *Be* and *Have* (pp. 100–103) *Underline the verb in parentheses that correctly completes each sentence.*

19. A forest (has, have) several layers.

20. Small trees and shrubs (is, are) close to the ground.

21. This forest (have, had) survived a fire.

Irregular Verbs (pp. 104–111) *Write the past form of the verb in parentheses to correctly complete each sentence.*

22. My classmates (speak) softly in the forest.   _____

23. Birds (fly) from branch to branch.   _____

24. Grass and ferns had (grow) on the forest floor.   _____

Contractions with *Not* (pp. 112–115) *Read each sentence. Write a contraction for each pair of words in* **boldface.**

25. Our trip **has not** gone too well.   _____

26. We **did not** become discouraged though.   _____

27. Our reports **will not** be due until next week.   _____

Verbs Often Misused (pp. 116–119) *Underline the word in parentheses that correctly completes each sentence.*

28. The rangers (leave, let) us take a rest.

29. We (sit, set) our notebooks on the ground.

30. We (teach, learn) more about the forest from the film.

Unit 3 Test

DIRECTIONS *Fill in the circle next to the sentence that spells and uses verbs or contractions correctly.*

1. ○ A storyteller sets by a campfire.
   ○ A crowd have gathered near her.
   ○ She is telling an old story now.
   ○ The story learns the people important truths.

2. ○ Our class discuss folktales.
   ○ Folktales werent written at first.
   ○ Storytellers speaked them aloud.
   ○ People wrote them down later.

3. ○ Children loves folktales.
   ○ The tales teach and entertain.
   ○ A folktale have more than one author.
   ○ The stories belongs to everyone.

4. ○ Folktales begun long ago.
   ○ Changes occured over the years.
   ○ Storytellers varyed the story in different ways.
   ○ There is more than one version of each folktale.

5. ○ Scholars collect folk stories long ago.
   ○ These scholars gone all over the world.
   ○ They recorded hundreds of versions of "Cinderella."
   ○ Scholars studyed these tales.

6. ○ Characters arent always people.
   ○ Fables have animal characters.
   ○ These animals acts like people.
   ○ Fables tryed to teach lessons.

7. ○ He bring me a book of legends.
   ○ Legends tell about real people.
   ○ The legend's details isn't always true.
   ○ Leave me tell you about King Arthur and his sword.

8. ○ Moviemakers have made many films from folktales.
   ○ I have went to many of them.
   ○ Thousands of folktales set on library shelves.
   ○ You could'nt find better stories!

DIRECTIONS *Read the paragraphs, and look carefully at each underlined part. Fill in the circle next to the answer choice that shows the correct spelling and use of verbs or contractions. If the underlined part is already correct, fill in the circle for "Correct as is."*

People <u>have sung</u> folk songs since long ago. Scholars do not know who
(9)
created most of the traditional folk songs. Singers <u>have droped some verses</u>
(10)
from the songs over the centuries. They <u>has simplifyed</u> some verses, too. They
(11)
have also sung the same words to different tunes. Singers taught these songs
to others, and <u>they chosed</u> to pass them on, too.
(12)
Sailors and cowhands <u>write and sung</u> songs to make the workday go
(13)
faster. Other folk songs focused on families, love, or nature. We still hear folk
songs today. This music often <u>express strong feelings and leaves</u> us see life in a
(14)
new way.

9. ◯ has sung
◯ have sang
◯ has sang
◯ Correct as is

10. ◯ has dropped some verses
◯ had droped some verses
◯ have dropped some verses
◯ Correct as is

11. ◯ have simplifyed
◯ has simplified
◯ have simplified
◯ Correct as is

12. ◯ they chosen
◯ they choose
◯ they chose
◯ Correct as is

13. ◯ written and sung
◯ wrote and sang
◯ wrote and sung
◯ Correct as is

14. ◯ express strong feelings and lets
◯ expresses strong feelings and leaves
◯ expresses strong feelings and lets
◯ Correct as is

Lesson 27: **Adjectives**

LEARN

■ An **adjective** is a word that describes a noun or a pronoun.

- An adjective can tell *what kind* or *how many*.

   Anna collects **unusual** instruments.
   She has **twelve** instruments in her collection.

- An adjective may come before the noun it describes or after a linking verb.

   Handmade instruments fascinate me.
   They are **unfamiliar** to **most** people.

- Two or more adjectives before a noun are usually separated by a comma. A comma is not used when one of the adjectives tells *how many*.

   Panpipes have a **soft, mellow** sound.
   They are made from **many wooden** tubes.

Panpipes

■ A **proper adjective** is an adjective formed from a proper noun. Like a proper noun, a proper adjective begins with a capital letter. Often the spelling changes.

PROPER NOUNS	China	Mexico	England
PROPER ADJECTIVES	**Chinese**	**Mexican**	**English**

Panpipes are a **South American** instrument.
She is playing a **Spanish** song.

PRACTICE

A   *Underline the adjective or adjectives that describe the noun in **boldface**.*

1. The didgeridoo is an Australian **instrument**.

2. It is made from a long, hollow **branch**.

3. The didgeridoo has a startling **sound**.

4. You often hear the koto in Japanese **music**.

5. The koto has fine, silky **strings**.

6. Many famous **musicians** in Japan play the koto.

7. Several Asian **instruments** have a similar sound.

8. The tubes or reeds in a panpipe have different **lengths**.

9. The ancient Greek **panpipe** is called a *syrinx*.

10. The Bolivian **people** call panpipes *zamponas*.

B *Underline the adjective or adjectives in each sentence once. Underline the noun that the adjective describes twice.*

1. The sansa is an African instrument.

2. The design is simple.

3. Its body is a hollow, wooden block.

4. Thin, metal strips are the keys.

5. Its sound is delightful.

6. Musicians play the sansa in many Kenyan villages.

7. Indian musicians invented the jalatarang.

8. This instrument consists of many different bowls filled with water.

9. A musician taps the bowls with a thin stick made of bamboo.

10. The jalatarang has a sweet tone.

11. Its notes are clear.

12. Some Mexican orchestras have included the jalatarang.

C *Write one or more adjectives to complete each sentence. Choose adjectives from the box, or use adjectives of your own. Do not use an adjective more than once.*

Remember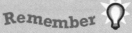
An **adjective** is a word that describes a noun or a pronoun. A **proper adjective** begins with a capital letter.

> beautiful   incredible   Mexican   sunny
>
> talented   three   traditional   warm

1. Our family went to a(n) _____ music festival last summer.

2. The festival was in a(n) _____ park near Toronto.

3. We enjoyed the amazing music for _____ days.

4. Fortunately, we had _____, _____ weather every day.

5. _____ performers from all over the world were playing

_____ folk music.

6. A brass band from Tijuana played _____ cowboy tunes.

> French   friendly   human
>
> rich   South American   steady

7. A guitarist from France sang _____ lullabies.

8. All the musicians were _____ to the audience.

9. Musicians from Peru, Chile, and other _____
countries played the panpipes.

10. I could hear the _____ rhythm of drums, too.

11. The world's musical heritage is so _____!

12. Music helps make us _____.

WRITE

Online For grammar games and activities, visit www.grammarworkshop.com.

You can improve your writing by combining two short, related sentences into a single sentence. One way to do this is to move the adjectives from one sentence into the other sentence. The combined sentence will sound smoother.

A bagpipe has five pipes. A bagpipe has wooden pipes.
A bagpipe has **five wooden** pipes.

D *Combine each pair of sentences by moving the adjective from one sentence into the other. The first one is done for you.*

1. A bagpipe's sound is unforgettable. The sound is strange. _____

   A bagpipe's strange sound is unforgettable.

2. Ancient Roman musicians played the bagpipes. Ancient Persian musicians did, too.

_____

3. Scottish bagpipers are well known today. So are Irish bagpipers. _____

_____

4. We listened to the loud instruments. We listened to the colorful instruments.

_____

5. The theremin is a modern instrument. It is electronic. _____

_____

6. A scientist invented the theremin in 1920. The scientist was Russian. _____

_____

7. A theremin has an antenna. The antenna is long. _____

_____

8. Musicians move their hands over the antenna to make sounds. The sounds are eerie.

_____

Go back to all the sentences you wrote.
Underline all of the adjectives in each sentence.

Lesson 28: **Articles and Demonstrative Adjectives**

LEARN

■ The special adjectives *a, an,* and *the* are called **articles**. *A* and *an* refer to **any** person, place, or thing. *The* refers to a **specific** person, place, or thing.

> Let's take **a** walk downtown. (any)
> **The** local history interests me. (specific)

- Use *a* before a singular noun that begins with a consonant sound.
  > **a** postcard

- Use *an* before a singular noun that begins with a vowel sound.
  > **an** editorial

- Use *the* to refer to singular or plural nouns.
  > **the** town   **the** monuments

■ *This, that, these,* and *those* are demonstrative adjectives. A **demonstrative adjective** tells *which one* and always comes before a noun.

- Use *this* (singular) and *these* (plural) to refer to people or things nearby.
  > **This** school was built in 1912.   **These** houses were built before 1850.

- Use *that* (singular) and *those* (plural) to refer to people or things farther away.
  > What was the name of **that** old railroad?
  > **Those** railroad tracks are no longer used.

- Do not use *here* or *there* after demonstrative adjectives.
  > **CORRECT**   **This** statue honors Lincoln.
  > **INCORRECT**   **This here** statue honors Lincoln.

PRACTICE

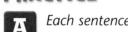 *Each sentence below may contain an article, a demonstrative adjective, or both. Underline each article once and each demonstrative adjective twice.*

1. Take a look at this book of photographs.

2. This photograph shows an engine pulling into town.

3. That old building was a shoe factory long ago.

4. Today, it is an aquarium with exhibits featuring aquatic animals.

5. Everywhere I look, I see a clue to the town's history.

6. Those houses across the river were built before 1920.

7. From the architecture, we know these houses are older.

8. There is the corner of Quarry Street and Granite Street.

9. Workers once cut huge blocks of granite stone in that area.

10. Let's keep walking and solve the mystery of this town's history.

B *Write the word in parentheses that correctly completes each sentence.*

1. _____ old postcards show our town long ago. (This, These)

2. Did you know our town once presented _____ opera? (a, an)

3. _____ photograph shows some trolley cars. (This, Those)

4. _____ trolley line ran through town until the 1930s. (A, An)

5. Can you read the cornerstone on _____ courthouse over there? (this, that)

6. Work on _____ town's courthouse must have begun in 1871. (the, an)

7. _____ little waterway is called Osage Creek. (This, These)

8. _____ town library has several books about local history. (The, An)

C *Dana created a slide show about her town's history. Part of the script for her slide show is given below. Dana made five mistakes using articles and five mistakes using demonstrative adjectives. Use the proofreading marks in the box to correct the errors.*

1. This photo was taken in 1940. Back in these days, our town had its own airfield. That there man is my great-grandfather at work on a airplane.

2. More than 30 trolley cars served our town between 1910 and 1941. The next picture shows the trolley car. The trolleys traveled on these tracks in the pavement. These here overhead electric wires provided the power.

3. This photo shows Center Street, the same road that runs through town today. In 1920, it was a dirt road with an maple tree every 10 feet alongside it. Those there trees were cut down when the road was widened in 1950.

4. Back in the 1920s and 1930s, our town had the picnic every June. I'm not sure who these here people in this picture are, but they must be having fun. The next picture was taken at a farm outside town called Oak Grove. Today, it's an modern housing development.

Proofreading Marks

∧	Add
⊙	Period
ℓ	Take out
≡	Capital letter
/	Small letter

Did you correct five mistakes with articles and five mistakes with demonstrative adjectives?

WRITE

Online For grammar games and activities, visit **www.grammarworkshop.com**.

D Write six questions about the history of your own community, city, or state. Use a demonstrative adjective (**this, that, these,** or **those**) in each question. Also, use the articles **a, an,** and **the** in some questions.

Examples: When was this community founded?
Who is that a statue of?

1. _____

_____

2. _____

_____

3. _____

_____

4. _____

_____

On the lines below, suggest two ways that you might find out the answers to your questions. Use articles and demonstrative adjectives in your answers.

5. _____

_____

6. _____

_____

Proofreading Checklist ✔

❑ Did you use the articles **a, an,** and **the** correctly?
❑ Did you use the demonstrative adjectives (**this, that, these,** and **those**) correctly?

Lesson 29: **Comparing with Adjectives**

LEARN

■ An **adjective** has different forms for comparing. Use either *-er* or *more* to compare two people, places, things, or ideas. Use either *-est* or *most* to compare more than two items.

- One-syllable adjectives and some two-syllable adjectives add *-er* or *-est*.

   Asian elephants are **smaller** than African elephants.
   Of all land mammals, elephants are **heaviest**.

- Always use *more* and *most* to compare adjectives with three or more syllables.

   Elephants are **more intelligent** than giraffes.
   Elephants are the **most enormous** land animals.

African elephants

■ When you add *-er* or *-est* to an adjective, the spelling may change.

Adjectives ending in *e*	tame tam**er** tam**est**
Adjectives ending in a consonant and *y*	busy bus**ier** bus**iest**
Adjectives ending in a single vowel and consonant	sad sad**der** sad**dest**

■ Do not use *-er* or *-est* together with *more* and *most*.

   INCORRECT   An African elephant's ears are **more larger** than an Asian elephant's.

   CORRECT   An African elephant's ears are **larger** than an Asian elephant's.

PRACTICE

A *In Column A, write the form of the adjective that compares two items. In Column B, write the form of the adjective that compares three items.*

A	B

1. dry _____   **3.** beautiful _____

2. glad _____   **4.** cute _____

	A			**B**	
5. natural	_____		**8.** wealthy	_____	
6. nice	_____		**9.** unbelievable	_____	
7. humorous	_____		**10.** wet	_____	

B *Write the form of the adjective in parentheses that correctly completes each sentence.*

1. Elephants are the _____ animals on Earth. (strong)

2. African elephants are _____ than Asian elephants. (fierce)

3. Female elephants are _____ on family members than male elephants. (dependent)

4. The _____ member of an elephant herd is a female. (respected)

5. The elephant's two _____ teeth are called tusks. (big)

6. One of the elephant's two tusks is usually _____ than the other. (short)

7. The skin inside an elephant's ear is _____ than the skin around most of its body. (thin)

8. Of the elephant's five senses, smell is the _____. (sensitive)

9. An elephant's hearing is _____ than its vision. (keen)

10. An elephant's heart is 50 times _____ than a human's heart. (heavy)

Asian elephants

C Michelle wrote a report about elephant intelligence. In this part of her report, she made seven mistakes using adjectives that compare. Use the proofreading marks in the box to correct the mistakes.

Elephants are more smarter than people realize.

For one thing, elephants are faster learners than other animals. They can be trained to do many tasks. Long ago, elephants were trained for war. War elephants were the frighteningest force on the battlefield. Elephants also did the heavy work in India and Southeast Asia in the days before tractors.

Elephants show intelligence with their emotions, too. They greet each other with a low rumble that gets more louder when they meet old friends. Long separations lead to the noisyest reunions.

Elephants also show sadness. Nothing is sader than losing a family member. Elephants might stand beside the body of a loved one for days.

Elephants also teach each other. The older ones, for example, will teach the more younger ones that the easyest places to dig for salt are caves.

Proofreading Marks

∧	Add
⊙	Period
ℓ	Take out
≡	Capital letter
/	Small letter

Did you correct seven mistakes with adjectives that compare?

WRITE

Online · For grammar games and activities, visit
www.grammarworkshop.com.

D *Follow the directions below to write groups of three sentences that compare the three species of rhinos listed in the chart. In your first sentence, use the adjective in parentheses. In your second sentence, compare two of the species. In your third sentence, compare all three species. Base your comparisons on the information in the chart.*

	Weight	Height (to shoulder)	Body Length
One-horned rhino	3300–4400 lb	5–6.5 ft	7–12 ft
White rhino	5000–8000 lb	5–6 ft	12–14 ft
Sumatran rhino	1300–1700 lb	3–5 ft	6.5–9 ft

1. Use the information about weight to compare the three species of rhinos. (heavy)

_____

_____

2. Use the information about height to compare the three species of rhinos. (tall)

_____

_____

3. Use the information about body length to compare the three species of rhinos. (long)

_____

_____

Proofreading Checklist ☑

❏ *Did you use the **-er** ending or **more** to compare two items?*
❏ *Did you use the **-est** ending or **most** to compare three items?*

Lesson 30: Comparing with *Good* and *Bad*

LEARN

■ The words *better* and *best* are the two forms of the adjective *good* that are used for comparing.

- Use *better* to compare two people, places, or things.

- Use *best* to compare more than two people, places, or things.
  Today is a **good** day for a parade.
  The weather is **better** today than yesterday.
  Today's weather is the **best** we've had all month.

■ The words *worse* and *worst* are the two forms of the adjective *bad* that are used for comparing.

- Use *worse* to compare two people, places, or things.

- Use *worst* to compare more than two people, places, or things.
  Yesterday's weather was **bad**.
  Last Monday's weather was **worse** than yesterday's.
  Of all the months, which month had the **worst** weather?

■ Do not use *-er* or *-est* or *more* or *most* when comparing with *good* and *bad*.

CORRECT   This year's parade is **better** than last year's.
INCORRECT   This year's parade is **gooder** than last year's.
INCORRECT   This year's parade is **more better** than last year's.

PRACTICE

A   *Write the adjective in parentheses that correctly completes each sentence.*

1. Of all the holidays, Memorial Day is the _____ day for a parade. (better, best)

2. The weather in late May is usually _____ than in early spring. (better, best)

3. This year, May's weather was _____ than April's. (worse, worst)

4. Attendance at the parade was the _____ it's ever been. (worse, worst)

5. The Lane Middle School band looked _____ this year than last year. (better, best)

6. Of all the instruments, the trumpets sounded _____. (better, best)

7. Even the drummers sounded _____. (good, best)

8. The band's marching at practice looked _____ because of the rain. (bad, worst)

9. The band's performance was _____ than that of the Howard Middle School band. (better, best)

10. Next year, the band hopes for _____ weather than it had this year. (better, best)

B *Write the form of the adjective in parentheses that correctly completes each sentence.*

1. I think that the Cub Scouts had the _____ float in the parade. (good)

2. They had done a really _____ job. (good)

3. The _____ view of the parade is from the stands along Main Street. (good)

4. My friends and I had the _____ seats of all. (bad)

5. The sound system was _____ than last year, so we couldn't hear. (bad)

6. A _____ thunderstorm interrupted the mayor's speech. (bad)

7. Everyone felt much _____ when the storm finally ended. (good)

8. All in all, the Memorial Day Parade was much _____ than I'd hoped. (good)

C Denzel wrote this personal narrative about what happened on Memorial Day. He made six mistakes using the forms of **good** and **bad**. Use the proofreading marks in the box to correct the errors.

Proofreading Marks

∧	Add
⊙	Period
℮	Take out
≡	Capital letter
/	Small letter

On Memorial Day, I had a bad headache. My school band was marching in the Memorial Day parade. This would prove to be my worstest parade ever!

I think I'm the goodest drummer in the school band. That day, however, I was not feeling or playing well.

My marching certainly looked sick. "Denzel!" the bandleader barked. "Get in step. You're a gooder marcher than that!" I had the baddest headache imaginable.

Later, the mayor gave a speech. "Why do we remember this day?" he began. My headache only got more worse.

Suddenly, I was lying on the ground. "Move away! Give him air!" someone shouted. I felt more better once cold water was splashed on my face.

"And that is why we remember this day!" I heard the mayor say. I would remember this day, too!

Did you correct six mistakes with forms of *good* and *bad*?

WRITE

D *Imagine your public library has been completely remodeled and is open for longer hours. Write sentences about three specific things you like about the new library. Use the adjectives **good**, **better**, and **best** in your sentences.*

1. _____

_____

2. _____

_____

3. _____

_____

*Now write three more sentences about the changes in your library. Tell about some things that you don't like very much. Use the words **bad**, **worse**, and **worst** in your sentences.*

4. _____

_____

5. _____

_____

6. _____

_____

Proofreading Checklist ☑

❑ *Did you use **good** and **bad** to describe one person, place, or thing?*

❑ *Did you use **better** and **worse** to compare two things?*

❑ *Did you use **best** and **worst** to compare more than two things?*

Lesson 31: **Adverbs**

LEARN

■ An **adverb** is a word that describes a verb, an adjective, or another adverb.

DESCRIBES A VERB   **Slowly,** the hot-air balloon rose.

DESCRIBES AN ADJECTIVE   The day was **very** windy.

DESCRIBES AN ADVERB   We soared **extremely** high!

■ Most adverbs tell *how, when,* or *where* an action takes place. Many adverbs end in *-ly.*
Notice that adverbs can come before or after the words they describe.

HOW	The balloon **easily** rose.
WHEN	**Recently,** we flew in the balloon.
WHERE	We flew the balloon **westward**.

Some adverbs answer the question *how much?*

HOW MUCH   We were **very** excited.

■ Here are some adverbs that tell *how, when, where,* and *how much.*

HOW	quietly	suddenly	slowly	together
WHEN	always	eventually	sometimes	soon
WHERE	far	nearby	south	there
HOW MUCH	extremely	quite	rather	very

PRACTICE

A   *In each sentence, circle the adverb that describes the verb, adjective, or adverb in **boldface**. Then write whether the adverb tells **how, when, where,** or **how much.** The first one is done for you.*

1. Our hot air balloon ride was (very) **exciting**.   _____how much_____

2. We arrived quite **early** for our ride.   _____

3. The balloon's burner **roared** loudly.   _____

4. Soon the huge balloon **filled** with hot air.   _____

5. My parents and I were rather **nervous**. _____

6. Carefully, we **climbed** into the big basket. _____

7. The captain warmly **welcomed** us. _____

8. Quickly, he **untied** the ropes. _____

9. The balloon moved extremely **smoothly**. _____

10. We **drifted** eastward in the brisk breeze. _____

B *Circle the adverb in each sentence. Then underline the word that the adverb describes.*

1. The balloon floated slowly over our town.

2. We drifted south toward the lake.

3. The flight was very smooth.

4. A flock of birds flew nearby.

5. We crossed Eagle Lake quickly.

6. The traffic on Route 88 crawled lazily.

7. Occasionally, we heard the balloon's burner.

8. It inflated the big balloon efficiently.

9. Suddenly, our captain began the descent.

10. The balloon descended rapidly.

11. The landing seemed completely effortless.

12. Let's go on another ride soon.

C *Write an adverb to complete each sentence. Choose an adverb from the box, or use an adverb of your own. The clue in parentheses will help you.*

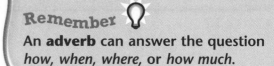

Remember
An **adverb** can answer the question *how, when, where,* or *how much.*

always	eventually	recently
bravely	finally	sometimes
carefully	frequently	soon
east	rapidly	very

1. Pascal Redding _____ loved adventure. (when)

2. Redding _____ completed an amazing trip around the world. (when)

3. Redding planned his solo trip _____. (how)

4. He checked weather reports _____. (when)

5. Redding took off from France and headed _____. (where)

6. Strong winds helped him move _____ over Asia and the Pacific. (how)

7. _____ South America was behind him, too. (when)

8. Redding _____ flew his balloon quite low. (when)

9. Redding was _____ lucky to avoid most storms. (how much)

10. _____, the balloon passed over the Atlantic Ocean. (when)

11. After 14 days, the balloon _____ landed in France again. (when)

12. Pascal Redding had _____ achieved his goal! (how)

WRITE

D *Adverbs can make sentences more interesting by telling* **how, when, where,** *and* **how much** *something happens. Read the paragraphs below. Add adverbs to complete the sentences. The adverbs should add details to the story.*

A hot-air balloon drifted _____ over Main Street.
(1)
A crowd gathered _____. "Will the balloon clear
(2)
those buildings?" someone asked _____. "Call the
(3)
fire department _____!" someone shouted.
(4)
Obviously, this was an emergency!

Two people in the balloon clutched the sides _____.
(5)
They glanced _____ at the telephone poles and
(6)
buildings below them. They were _____ terrified.
(7)
The balloon fell _____.
(8)
The pilot of the balloon worked _____ at
(9)
the heater. Something was _____ wrong with it.
(10)
The pilot could not get the heater to work _____.
(11)
_____, a gust of wind caught the balloon. The
(12)
wind lifted the balloon above the buildings. The crowd breathed

a sigh of relief.

Lesson 32: Comparing with Adverbs

LEARN

An **adverb** can compare two or more actions. Use the correct form of an adverb when you compare.

- When an adverb is a one-syllable word, add *-er* or *-est* to compare.

  - Add *-er* to most one-syllable adverbs to compare two actions.

  - Add *-est* to most one-syllable adverbs to compare more than two actions.
    Pat swims **faster** than I do.
    Of all the swimmers on the team, Nicky swims **fastest**.

- When the adverb is a word with two or more syllables, use the word *more* or *most* for comparing.

  - Use *more* with adverbs to compare two actions.

  - Use *most* with adverbs to compare more than two actions.
    Pat swims **more** often than I do.
    Of all the team members, Chris swims **most** often.

Adverbs ending in *-ly* also use the word *more* or *most* for comparing.

  Jackie starts the race **more** explosively than I do.
  Robin is the racer who reacts **most** explosively to the starter's whistle.

- When comparing, either add *-er* or *-est* to the adverb, or use *more* or *most*. Do not use *more* or *most* with *-er* or *-est*.

  INCORRECT   Lee jumps **more higher** than I do.
  CORRECT   Lee jumps **higher** than I do.

PRACTICE

A *Write the word in parentheses that correctly completes each sentence.*

1. I usually arrive at the pool _____ than Coach Stevens. (earlier, earliest)

2. Of all the swimmers on the team, I live _____ to the pool. (closer, closest)

3. My friend Jamie gets there _____ than I do.
(later, latest)

4. On our team, Jessie is the person who dives _____.
(more expertly, most expertly)

5. Jessie also practices _____ than I do.
(more regularly, most regularly)

6. I swim _____ in practice than in a swim meet.
(more slowly, most slowly)

7. Of all the sports, you use oxygen _____ when
swimming. (more rapidly, most rapidly)

8. A swimmer breathes _____ than a baseball
player. (more deeply, most deeply)

9. Before you swim, stretch your muscles _____ than
you are doing now. (more thoroughly, most thoroughly)

10. Of all my activities, I work _____ at swimming.
(harder, hardest)

B *Write the form of the adverb in parentheses that correctly
completes each sentence.*

1. Of all the swimming strokes, people swim _____
doing the crawl. (fast)

2. Most swimmers learn the crawl _____ than the
backstroke. (easily)

3. Of the four basic kicks, your legs move _____ in
the flutter kick. (rapidly)

4. Swimmers use the flutter kick _____ than the
dolphin kick. (often)

5. Of all our coaches, Coach Stevens has served _____.
(long)

C *In his journal, Eduardo wrote how he feels about diving. He made seven mistakes when using adverbs that compare. Use the proofreading marks in the box to correct the mistakes.*

Most people watch diving competitions more closely than they watch swimming meets. They also cheer most loudly for the divers than for the swimmers.

I have been swimming more long than I've been diving. A lot of people can swim more fast than I do, but diving emphasizes technique over speed. Of all the swimmers on our team, I work most hard at diving techniques. Two years ago, of all the kids at the pool, I dived most clumsily. This year, I am diving gracefullier than they are.

Every dive includes certain actions that you must follow while in the air. The most carefully you follow them, the better you will dive.

Diving is safe for properly trained athletes. Without good coaching and techniques, you can be injured most seriously than you realize. The more you train, the more expertly you will dive.

Proofreading Marks

∧	Add
⊙	Period
ℓ	Take out
≡	Capital letter
/	Small letter

Did you correct seven mistakes with adverbs that compare?

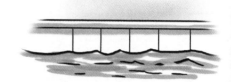

Online For grammar games and activities, visit
www.grammarworkshop.com.

WRITE

D Choose a sports game that you like and know well. Then make up
a play-by-play description of a game. Using the five points below,
write sentences in which you compare the actions of two or more players
during the game. In each sentence, use an adverb that compares. The first
one is done for you.

1. the accuracy of the players' throws or kicks _____

   Luis throws the football more accurately than Jed. _____

2. the speed of the players _____

_____

3. the frequency of the scoring _____

_____

4. the behavior of the players toward their opponents _____

_____

5. the behavior of the players toward the referees _____

_____

*Write two sentences of your own that compare two or more players
in the same sport or in different sports.*

6. _____

_____

7. _____

_____

Proofreading Checklist ✓

❑ *Did you use an adverb to compare the actions of two or
more players?*

❑ *Did you add **-er** or **more** to compare two actions?*

❑ *Did you add **-est** or **most** to compare more than two actions?*

Lesson 33: Using *Good* and *Well*, *Real* and *Very*

LEARN

The words *good, well, real,* and *very* are often used incorrectly. To use these words correctly, think carefully about what you are describing.

- *Good* is an adjective that describes a noun.

   Grandma Moses was a **good** artist.

Well is usually an adverb that describes a verb. It answers the question *how.*

   Her paintings sell **well** today.

Well is an adjective when it means "healthy."

   Even at age 100, she felt **well** enough to paint.

- *Real* is an adjective that describes a noun. *Real* means "actual."

   Moses's paintings show **real** scenes from her life.

Very is an adverb that describes an adjective or another adverb. *Very* means "extremely."

   Critics were **very** happy with Moses's paintings.
   Grandma Moses painted each scene **very** carefully.

PRACTICE

A *Underline the word that good, well, real, or very decribes.*

1. Grandma Moses is a **good** example of a self-taught artist.

2. Her **real** name was Anna Robertson Moses.

3. She was not **very** interested in art until she was 77.

4. Her large family and farm had kept her **very** busy until then.

5. Her paintings showed **real** places from her childhood.

6. Even in her eighties and nineties, she remembered these scenes **well**.

7. At first, her neighbors didn't think **well** of her paintings.

8. Art critics understood that she was a **real** artist.

9. **Very** large museums bought and showed her paintings.

10. A painting by Grandma Moses is **very** valuable today.

B *Write the word in parentheses that correctly completes each sentence.*

1. Even as a child, Georgia O'Keeffe had a _____ desire to become an artist. (real, very)

2. _____ few American women were artists in the early 1900s. (Real, Very)

3. O'Keeffe went to several _____ art schools. (good, well)

4. She did _____ in her classes, too. (good, well)

5. O'Keeffe developed a _____ love for the desert. (real, very)

6. Her early scenes of New Mexico look _____ mysterious. (real, very)

7. She had painted these landscapes _____. (well, good)

8. O'Keeffe was becoming a _____ successful artist. (real, very)

9. In later years, she became _____ famous for her paintings of desert rocks. (real, very)

10. Her paintings of dried bones and exotic flowers are especially

_____. (good, well)

11. The desert climate kept Georgia O'Keeffe feeling _____. (good, well)

12. Even in her nineties, she continued to paint _____. (good, well)

C. *Anna wrote a report about another American artist, Mary Cassatt. In these paragraphs from the report, she made three mistakes when using **good** and **well**, and four mistakes when using **real** and **very**. Use the proofreading marks in the box to correct these seven mistakes.*

Proofreading Marks

∧	Add
⊙	Period
ℒ	Take out
≡	Capital letter
/	Small letter

Very few women in the nineteenth century painted as good as Mary Cassatt. As a young girl in Pennsylvania, she was real determined to become an artist. Her parents, however, had no real appreciation of art. They did not think a woman could succeed as an artist.

Mary Cassatt was determined. Not many women in 1861 went to the Pennsylvania Academy of Fine Arts. Mary Cassatt, however, did very good as a student there. Later, like many good artists, she sailed to France for more study.

In her best paintings, Mary Cassatt showed real people doing everyday tasks. The artist became real famous for her pictures of mothers and children. Many pictures show her family members. She painted these people especially good.

Mary Cassatt experimented with color and brushstrokes. She became real good friends with many great artists. She was real proud to be the only American artist in the French Impressionist exhibit in Paris.

Terra Foundation for American Art, Chicago/Art Resource, NY.

Did you find and correct four mistakes with *real* and *very*? Did you find and correct three mistakes with *good* and *well*?

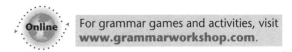

Online For grammar games and activities, visit
www.grammarworkshop.com.

Write Your Own

WRITE

D *Write about a favorite painting or photograph that you have seen. First, write two or three sentences about the details you can see in the painting or photograph. Then write two or three sentences telling whether you like the painting or photograph, and why. Use the words **real** or **very** in two sentences. Use the words **well** or **good** in two sentences as well.*

_____

_____

_____

_____

_____

_____

_____

_____

_____

_____

_____

_____

_____

_____

_____

Proofreading Checklist ☑

❏ *Did you use **good** and **real** to describe nouns?*
❏ *Did you use **well** to describe verbs and **very** to describe adjectives or other adverbs?*

Lesson 34: Negatives

LEARN

- Words that mean "no" are **negatives**. The words *no, not, nothing, none, never, no one, nowhere,* and *nobody* are negatives. Contractions with *not,* such as *aren't, doesn't,* and *haven't,* are also negatives. The word *not* is an adverb.

  Before 1880, there were **no** cars.
  No one had invented the automobile.
  Cars **weren't** popular until later.

- A negative idea is expressed by using one negative word. Do not use a double negative.

Model T Ford

INCORRECT	**None** of the cars had **no** tops.
CORRECT	**None** of the cars had tops.
CORRECT	**None** of the cars had **any** tops.

Look at the sentences above. Notice how a sentence with a double negative can be corrected. You can drop a negative word or change one of the negative words to a positive word.

Negative Words	Positive Words
no, none, nothing	any, anything
never	ever
no one, nobody	anyone, anybody
nowhere	anywhere

PRACTICE

A *Write the negative word in each sentence.*

1. A hundred years ago, no one believed cars would replace horses. _____

2. Back then, nine out of ten roads weren't paved. _____

3. Nobody could avoid deep mud and dust. _____

4. None of the early cars were very reliable.   _____

5. Breakdowns and accidents never seemed to end.   _____

6. States had no tests for new drivers.   _____

7. Gas stations were nowhere to be found.   _____

8. Car heaters hadn't been invented.   _____

9. Early autos seemed to be nothing but trouble.   _____

10. The saying "Get a horse!" was not a joke in those days. _____

B *Write the word in parentheses that correctly completes each sentence.*

1. In 1900, most Americans couldn't afford (no, any) kind of car.   _____

2. Nobody but rich people (never, ever) bought cars.   _____

3. Henry Ford's factory (was, wasn't) nothing like
other factories.   _____

4. Ford's Model T cars cost (no, any) more than $500.   _____

5. No one (could, couldn't) resist those prices!   _____

6. His factory didn't (never, ever) stop making new cars.   _____

7. Soon you couldn't go (nowhere, anywhere) without seeing cars.   _____

8. Gas stations appeared where (none, any) had existed before.   _____

9. With paved highways, it was no problem driving
(nowhere, anywhere).   _____

10. There (was, wasn't) no end to the new gadgets in cars either.   _____

11. Many Americans wouldn't drive (anything, nothing)
but a big car.   _____

12. They didn't have (any, no) worries about the cost of gasoline.   _____

C Lena wrote an essay about three problems with today's cars. She used eight double negatives in her writing. Use the proofreading marks in the box to correct the mistakes.

Proofreading Marks

∧	Add
⊙	Period
ℒ	Take out
≡	Capital letter
/	Small letter

Americans probably won't never give up their cars, so three serious car problems must be solved.

One problem is gas prices. No one never thought gas would get so expensive. Someday, there won't be no more oil. We need to develop other fuels to run our cars.

Car safety is a challenge, too. In the past, cars didn't have no seatbelts. There weren't no airbags or nothing else to protect you in a crash. Even today's safer cars have not put an end to injuries.

Air pollution is a third problem. Until recent years, no one did nothing about car exhaust. Even though car engines haven't never burned cleaner than they do now, car exhaust still causes air pollution today.

Did you correct eight double negatives?

Online For grammar games and activities, visit **www.grammarworkshop.com**.

WRITE

D Look at each traffic sign below. Write a complete sentence that tells what the sign means. Try to use a different negative word in each sentence. The first one is done for you.

SPEED LIMIT 35

1. No one can drive faster than 35 miles per hour here.

2. _____

3. _____

4. _____

5. _____

6. _____

7. _____

Proofreading Checklist ☑

❏ *Did you use a different negative word in each sentence?*
❏ *Did you avoid using a double negative?*

Lesson 35: **Prepositions**

LEARN

■ A **preposition** is a word that relates a noun or pronoun to some other word in the sentence.

>   Mammoth Cave is **in** southwest Kentucky.

Here are some common prepositions:

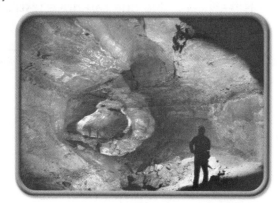

about	below	in	over
above	beneath	inside	through
across	beside	into	throughout
after	between	near	to
along	by	of	under
around	down	off	until
at	during	on	with
before	for	out	without
behind	from	outside	

■ The **object of the preposition** is the noun or pronoun that follows a preposition.

>   **During** our **vacation**, we visited the cave.
>   Mammoth Cave has 350 miles **of** mapped **trails**.
>   All **of us** joined a tour.

PRACTICE

A *Underline the preposition in each sentence.*

1. You can enter several connected caves below the surface.

2. Mammoth Cave is the longest cave in the world.

3. Its temperature is always about 54°F.

4. Dripping water slowly carved the caves from limestone rock.

5. Underground rivers run through the caves.

6. Native Americans first entered Mammoth Cave during prehistoric times.

7. They explored the space inside the cave.

8. By 1799, Kentucky settlers had discovered the cave.

9. Mammoth Cave offers many tours for today's visitors.

10. Guides warn you never to write on the cave walls.

B *Underline the preposition in each sentence. Then write the object of the preposition on the line.*

1. Throughout the cave, you can see amazing sights. _____

2. Electric lights show stalactites hanging from the ceilings. _____

3. They resemble giant icicles above your head. _____

4. Cone-shaped stalagmites are on the floor. _____

5. Seeing them sent shivers down my spine. _____

6. Minerals form shapes along the walls. _____

7. The largest one is named after Niagara Falls. _____

8. Water dripping into the cave has carved deep pits. _____

9. During the day, countless bats rest there. _____

10. At night, the bats leave the cave. _____

11. Fish without eyes swim underground. _____

12. Some tours let you crawl, climb, and squeeze through tight spaces. _____

Write a preposition to complete each sentence. Choose a preposition from the box, or use a preposition of your own.

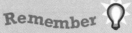

Remember

A **preposition** relates a noun or pronoun to some other word in the sentence.

across	during	in	on
around	for	inside	with
by	from	of	without

1. An exciting hobby _____ cave lovers is spelunking.

2. Spelunkers should always explore caves _____ a group.

3. These groups should be led _____ an experienced leader.

4. It is easy to get lost _____ a cave.

5. Accurate maps _____ a cave are essential.

6. _____ maps, spelunkers wouldn't know what lies ahead.

7. Spelunkers wear lamps _____ their helmets.

8. A flashlight _____ one hand is also necessary.

9. Rubber boots let spelunkers walk _____ shallow streams.

10. _____ the visit, a spelunker should not damage any rock formations.

11. Spelunkers shouldn't remove anything _____ a cave either.

12. They should simply enjoy the amazing underground space

_____ them.

Online — For grammar games and activities, visit **www.grammarworkshop.com**.

WRITE

D *Imagine that you are standing deep inside a cave. It is totally dark all around you. Then you turn on your flashlight and the light attached to your helmet. Write six sentences about what you might experience in the cave. Include at least one preposition in each sentence. You may write about the topics in the box or choose your own topics.*

What you see	Where you are standing
What you hear	What you are wearing
What you feel	What you are thinking
What you smell	Who is with you

1. _____

_____

2. _____

_____

3. _____

_____

4. _____

_____

5. _____

_____

6. _____

_____

Proofreading Checklist ☑

❏ *Does each sentence tell about what you might experience in a cave?*

❏ *Did you use a preposition in each sentence?*

Lesson 36: **Prepositional Phrases**

LEARN

- A **prepositional phrase** is a group of words that begins with a preposition and ends with its object. The object is the noun or pronoun that follows the preposition.

  under the tree   beneath the rock
  along the edge   near me

A prepositional phrase includes a preposition, the object of the preposition, and all the words between them. A prepositional phrase can be at the beginning, in the middle, or at the end of a sentence.

On Saturday, we attended a poetry reading.
Many people **in our community** write poems.
Bob wrote a poem **about the moonlit sky.**

- A prepositional phrase may have a compound (more than one) object.

  You can find poems **in books and magazines**.
  This poetry book is a gift **for Jack and her**.

PRACTICE

A *Underline the prepositional phrase in each sentence.*

1. She read aloud a poem about two horses.

2. The images in the poem are very beautiful.

3. During her reading, I imagined the scene.

4. That poem had a strong effect on me.

5. After the reading, I wrote my own poem.

6. The words of a poem sound special.

7. The last words in some lines often rhyme.

8. With rhythm and rhyme, poems sound musical.

9. Within a poem, you will find comparisons.

10. A poet might compare a person to the moon and stars.

B *In each sentence, underline the prepositional phrase once. Underline the object (or objects) of the preposition twice. The first one is done for you.*

1. Many poems are <u>about nature</u>.

2. Natural beauty is all around us.

3. In a poet's imagination, a snowflake becomes a diamond.

4. The wind whispers through the trees and grass.

5. Above the purple sky, the stars shine brightly.

6. The poet creates images for readers and listeners.

7. Some words and images arrive without much effort.

8. Usually, poets search hard for the right words.

9. A poem is a unique gift from a poet.

10. With a little imagination, a reader can open that gift.

11. Readers must spot the images behind the words and lines.

12. They must hear the repeated sounds across the lines.

C *Write a prepositional phrase to complete each sentence. Choose a prepositional phrase from the box, or use a prepositional phrase of your own.*

for the right moment	above the city	below the plane
along the plane's path	from the tower	at the gate
with a gentle thump	for the landing	around the city
with their pointed towers	among the clouds	in the darkness

1. _____, a jumbo jet waits to land.

2. Like a giant bird, the plane circles lazily _____.

3. The pilot must wait _____ to begin the landing.

4. _____, the skyscrapers' lights glitter like diamonds.

5. These buildings, _____, seem to stretch upward.

6. Far below, the cars crawl slowly _____.

7. _____, the streetlights shine.

8. Finally, a signal flashes _____.

9. The time _____ is now!

10. The buildings _____ tremble.

11. _____, the jet touches down.

12. Now the jumbo jet rests silently _____.

WRITE

 Combining Sentences

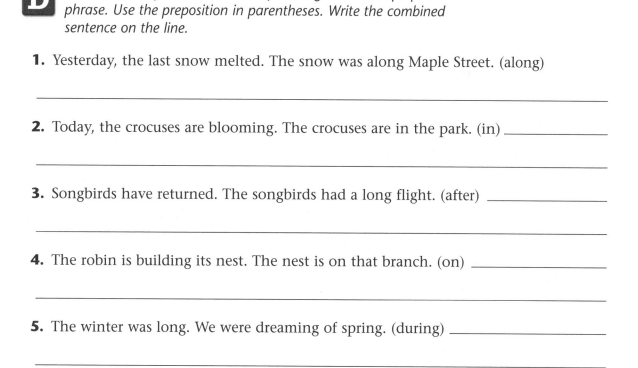

Online · For grammar games and activities, visit **www.grammarworkshop.com**.

You can improve your writing by combining two short, related sentences. Sometimes you can turn one sentence into a prepositional phrase and add it to the other sentence.

RELATED SENTENCES	Each student must write a poem. The poem must be about a season.
COMBINED	Each student must write a poem **about a season**.

You may need to change the wording of a sentence in order to use a prepositional phrase.

RELATED SENTENCES	Spring is my favorite season. Spring has many beautiful sights.
COMBINED	**With so many beautiful sights**, spring is my favorite season.

D *Combine each pair of sentences by turning one into a prepositional phrase. Use the preposition in parentheses. Write the combined sentence on the line.*

1. Yesterday, the last snow melted. The snow was along Maple Street. (along)

_____

2. Today, the crocuses are blooming. The crocuses are in the park. (in) _____

_____

3. Songbirds have returned. The songbirds had a long flight. (after) _____

_____

4. The robin is building its nest. The nest is on that branch. (on) _____

_____

5. The winter was long. We were dreaming of spring. (during) _____

_____

Look Back Go back to the sentences you wrote. Underline the prepositional phrases in the sentences.

Adjectives (pp. 124–127) *Underline all the adjectives in each sentence.*

1. Canada is large and beautiful.

2. Many Canadians speak two languages.

3. Most people speak the French language in Quebec.

Articles and Demonstrative Adjectives (pp. 128–131)
Underline the word in parentheses that correctly completes each sentence.

4. (These, Those) maps in my hand show Canada.

5. Ottawa is (a, the) capital of Canada.

6. (This, These) territory in the north is the Yukon.

Comparing with Adjectives (pp. 132–135) *Write the form of the adjective in parentheses that correctly completes each sentence.*

7. Canada is (big) than the United States. _____

8. Of the ten provinces, Quebec is (large). _____

9. Ontario is (crowded) than Quebec. _____

Comparing with *Good* and *Bad* (pp. 136–139) *Write the form of the adjective in parentheses that correctly completes each sentence.*

10. My knowledge of Canada is (good) now than
    it was before. _____

11. Of all the provinces we visited, Nova Scotia
    had the (good) fishing. _____

12. In Quebec, my French was (bad) than Jon's. _____

Adverbs (pp. 140–143) *Circle the adverb in each sentence.*

13. The French were the European settlers who reached Canada first.

14. They quickly built a network of fur trading posts.

15. Canadian explorers and settlers moved westward.

Comparing with Adverbs (pp. 144–147) *Write the form of the adverb in parentheses that correctly completes each sentence.*

16. Canada grew (rapidly) in the 1800s than in the 1700s. _____

17. Of all its regions, the western areas were settled (slowly). _____

18. British Columbia was formed (early) than Manitoba. _____

Using *Good* and *Well*, *Real* and *Very* (pp. 148–151) *Underline the word in parentheses that correctly completes each sentence.*

19. Canada's prairies have (real, very) fertile soil.

20. Wheat and other grains grow (good, well) there.

21. Natural resources are one of Canada's (real, very) strengths.

Negatives (pp. 152–155) *Underline the word in parentheses that correctly completes each sentence.*

22. Huge areas in the north have (never, ever) been settled.

23. In these parts of Canada, you never see (no one, anyone).

24. You can't grow (anything, nothing) in the cold climate there.

Prepositions and Prepositional Phrases (pp. 156–163) *Underline the prepositional phrase in each sentence. Then circle the preposition.*

25. Canada's southern border stretches about 3000 miles.

26. In the eastern provinces, fishing villages dot the Atlantic coast.

27. The ports and cities on the Pacific Coast are amazing.

DIRECTIONS *Fill in the circle next to the sentence that spells and uses adjectives, adverbs, and negatives correctly.*

1. ○ Today is the busyest day at the diner.
   ○ It is more crowded today than it was on Sunday.
   ○ There is a real big crowd here.
   ○ I haven't never seen so many people.

2. ○ Dad opened earlyer today than usual.
   ○ There isn't no one waiting for a table.
   ○ Those booths by the door are all full.
   ○ Business is best this year than last.

3. ○ Dad is making french toast.
   ○ Mom takes orders most quickly than I do.
   ○ She tells Dad to hurry with that eggs.
   ○ Of the three cooks, Dad moves fastest.

4. ○ Clam chowder is our bigest seller.
   ○ This soup tastes more delicious of all.
   ○ We have the best soups in the city.
   ○ Mom is using a enormous ladle.

5. ○ Aunt Emma waits patiently for a order.
   ○ The man asks which dishes taste well.
   ○ He can't never decide what to eat.
   ○ My aunt says everything is good here.

6. ○ This here corner is the most crowded.
   ○ There isn't no way to move around.
   ○ Uncle Sy is slicing american cheese.
   ○ Dad is cooking a Spanish omelet.

7. ○ A customer asks for real orange juice.
   ○ Mom says the juice tastes real good.
   ○ There isn't nothing like orange juice.
   ○ It will help when you don't feel good.

8. ○ Dad never wanted to do nothing else.
   ○ He serves real good food.
   ○ He is the famousest cook in town.
   ○ His Irish stew is better than the soup.

DIRECTIONS *Read the paragraphs, and look carefully at each*
underlined part. Fill in the circle next to the answer choice that
shows the correct use and spelling of adjectives and negatives. If the
underlined part is already correct, fill in the circle of "Correct as is."

    Table-service restaurants are common all across our country. In <u>this types</u>
$\hspace{11.5cm}$ (9)
<u>of restaurants</u>, a waiter takes the order and brings the food to the table.
$\hspace{0.5cm}$ (9)
Family restaurants are the <u>most popularest</u> type of table-service restaurants.
$\hspace{4cm}$ (10)
Most ethnic restaurants are also table-service restaurants. You will often be

served <u>vietnamese, italian, or mexican</u> dishes in these restaurants.
$\hspace{2.5cm}$ (11)
    By contrast, fast-food restaurants specialize in serving food more quickly.

<u>These restaurants</u> provide <u>inexpensiver</u> food than table-service restaurants.
$\hspace{0.6cm}$ (12) $\hspace{3cm}$ (13)
Food experts say that fast food is the <u>most worst</u> kind of food because it is so
$\hspace{6.5cm}$ (14)
high in fat and salt.

9. ○ those type of restaurants
   ○ that types of restaurants
   ○ these types of restaurants
   ○ Correct as is

10. ○ more popular
    ○ most popular
    ○ more popularer
    ○ Correct as is

11. ○ Vietnamese, italian, or Mexican
    ○ vietnamese, Italian, or Mexican
    ○ Vietnamese, Italian, or Mexican
    ○ Correct as is

12. ○ These here
    ○ This
    ○ Those there
    ○ Correct as is

13. ○ inexpensivest
    ○ more inexpensive
    ○ most inexpensive
    ○ Correct as is

14. ○ worst
    ○ baddest
    ○ worser
    ○ Correct as is

Lesson 37: **Subject Pronouns**

LEARN

■ A **subject pronoun** takes the place of a noun or nouns in the subject of a sentence.

> Last summer, **Juan** went to Florida.
> **He** hiked in a park there.

> **Uncle Luis and Aunt Sonia** took Juan on the trip.
> **They** hiked many miles.

I, he, she, and *it* are singular subject pronouns. *We* and *they* are plural subject pronouns. *You* can be singular or plural.

■ In a sentence, the subject pronoun and the present-tense verb must agree in number. If the subject pronoun is *he, she,* or *it,* use a singular verb. If the subject pronoun is *I, we, you,* or *they,* use a plural verb. Many verbs with an *-s* at the end are singular and without the *-s* are plural.

- Add *-s* or *-es* to a verb if the subject pronoun is *he, she,* or *it.* If the verb ends in *y,* change the *y* to *i* before adding *-es.*
  She studies a map of Everglades National Park.
  It stretches across Florida's southern tip.

- Do not add *-s* or *-es* if the subject pronoun is *I, we, you,* or *they.*
  I enjoy hiking. **You like** hiking, too.
  Sometimes **we carry** cameras with us.
  They photograph the colorful birds and animals.

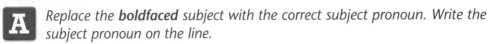

PRACTICE

A   *Replace the **boldfaced** subject with the correct subject pronoun. Write the subject pronoun on the line.*

1. **The Everglades** is a low, flat plain.   _____

2. **Summer storms** turn the plain into a grassy river.   _____

3. Aunt Sonia photographs a great blue heron. _____

4. Many tropical wading birds live in the Everglades. _____

5. Juan spots three tiny alligators in the water. _____

6. Uncle Luis and I photograph the baby reptiles. _____

7. Mrs. Dunn tells us about endangered species. _____

8. The Florida panther is in danger of dying out. _____

9. Scientists and conservationists try to protect
the Everglades and its animals. _____

10. Aunt Sonia, Juan, and I volunteer to help. _____

B *Write the present-tense form of the verb in parentheses to correctly complete each sentence.*

1. We _____ Florida's Kennedy Space Center. (visit)

2. It _____ a view of the future. (provide)

3. He _____ the takeoff of the Space Shuttle. (witness)

4. It _____ seven astronauts into space. (launch)

5. They _____ equipment up to the International
Space Station. (carry)

6. It _____ like silver in the sunlight. (flash)

7. She _____ until it disappears from view. (watch)

8. He _____ on a space suit at the space museum. (try)

9. You _____ a picture of the astronaut. (snap)

10. He _____ into the space flight simulator. (hurry)

11. I _____ a rock from the moon. (touch)

12. We _____ the Space Shuttle Explorer. (tour)

C *During his trip to Florida, Juan wrote a letter home. In it, he made six mistakes in subject-verb agreement. Use the proofreading marks to correct Juan's mistakes.*

Dear Mom,

I'm having a wonderful time in Florida with Aunt Sonia and Uncle Luis! We wishes you were here, too!

On Monday, we drove across the Seven-Mile Bridge. It cross about 7 miles of ocean, and it stretch from the Middle Keys to the Lower Keys. I'm glad I remembered from Social Studies class that a key is an island.

Key West is the most southern city in the United States. It occupy a beautiful coral island about 100 miles from the mainland. We had a great time there!

Today, we will cross the Seven-Mile Bridge again to go back to Miami. In some places, you drives really close to the water. It feel like you're sailing!

Love,

Juan

Proofreading Marks	
∧	Add
⊙	Period
℘	Take out
≡	Capital letter
/	Small letter

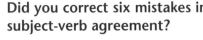

Did you correct six mistakes in subject-verb agreement?

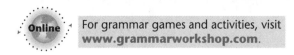

WRITE

Writing sounds awkward when the same nouns are repeated again and again.

> Juan visited Florida's biggest lake, Lake Okeechobee. Lake Okeechobee covers more than 700 square miles. Juan liked seeing the lake, but Juan was surprised that Lake Okeechobee is only 9 feet deep.

To improve this paragraph, you can replace some of the repeated nouns with subject pronouns. Be careful, though. Don't use the same pronoun too many times.

> Juan visited Florida's biggest lake, Lake Okeechobee. It covers more than 700 square miles. Juan liked seeing the lake, but he was surprised that it is only 9 feet deep.

D *Improve each paragraph by replacing two or more repeated nouns with subject pronouns. Write the revised paragraphs.*

1. Florida's orange groves are famous. Florida's orange groves provide Americans with most of their favorite juice. Juan and Uncle Luis visited an orange grove. Juan and Uncle Luis also bought grapefruit in another grove.

_____

_____

_____

2. Aunt Sonia and Juan went to St. Augustine, Florida. St. Augustine, Florida, is the oldest city in the United States. Aunt Sonia hurried to see the Castillo de San Marcos. Aunt Sonia had heard how beautiful the Castillo de San Marcos is.

_____

_____

_____

Go back to the paragraphs you wrote. Underline the subject pronouns you used to replace the repeated nouns.

Lesson 38: **Object Pronouns**

LEARN

■ A **subject pronoun** takes the place of a noun in the subject of a sentence. An **object pronoun** takes the place of a noun that is a direct object or the object of a preposition. An object pronoun follows an action verb.

DIRECT OBJECT
Mom drove **Alex** to the library.
Mom drove **him** to the library.

OBJECT OF PREPOSITION
The librarian handed some books to **Maria**.
The librarian handed some books to **her**.

■ The pronouns *me, him, her,* and *it* are singular object pronouns. The pronouns *us* and *them* are plural object pronouns. The pronoun *you* can be singular or plural.

■ *You* and *it* can be either subject pronouns or object pronouns.

SUBJECT PRONOUN   **You** like to read.
OBJECT PRONOUN   I admire **you** for reading.

SUBJECT PRONOUN   **It** is a great book.
OBJECT PRONOUN   Tony will read **it**.

PRACTICE

A   *Underline the pronoun in each sentence. Then write **subject pronoun** or **object pronoun** to tell what kind of pronoun it is.*

1. Here is a book for you.   _____

2. It is called *A Wrinkle in Time* by Madeleine L'Engle.   _____

3. You will like the main character, Meg Murray.   _____

4. Meg's father is missing, and Meg looks for him.   _____

5. She travels through space and time.   _____

6. Meg's brother and friend go with her.   _____

7. Many exciting things happen to them on the trip.   _____

8. My teacher read *A Wrinkle in Time* aloud to us.   _____

9. Then my teacher gave the book to me to put away.   _____

10. Everybody begged her to read the story again.   _____

B *Write the pronoun in parentheses that correctly completes each sentence.*

1. The librarian showed _____ books by Jean George. (we, us)

2. *My Side of the Mountain* is a book by _____. (she, her)

3. _____ liked the main character. (We, Us)

4. _____ will probably like him, too. (You, Him)

5. Sam Gribley amazed _____. (I, me)

6. _____ finds what he needs in the forest. (He, Him)

7. Sam finds wild plants and cooks _____. (they, them)

8. _____ would like to live like Sam! (I, Me)

9. *The Talking Earth* was another good book for _____. (I, me)

10. Billie Wind is the main character, and I'll never forget _____. (she, her)

11. _____ lives with the Seminole people. (She, Her)

12. Billie leaves _____ for a few days. (they, them)

13. A young Seminole boy helps _____. (she, her)

14. _____ and Billie survive a terrible hurricane. (He, Him)

15. This book teaches _____ about the environment. (we, us)

C Sunita wrote this book review of *The Skirt* by Gary Soto. In her review, she used six pronouns incorrectly. Read Sunita's book review, and find the mistakes. Use the proofreading marks in the box to correct those mistakes.

Miata Ramirez has a problem. Her has lost a treasured *folklorico* skirt. Miata's mother had given it to Miata to wear in a folk dance at church.

On Friday, Miata took the skirt to school. On the way home, she left it on the bus. What will Miata's parents say if they find out? Them might get angry.

On Saturday, Miata and Ana peek into all the buses at the school bus parking lot. The skirt has to be in one of they. Then Miata gets locked inside a bus. Now the girls are trapped in the lot! Miata's father is working nearby, and she spots he. Maybe he will see her, too.

The Skirt is a lot of fun and has a good ending. It teaches we a good lesson, too. Your family can help you with your problems. Trying to solve they on your own can cause bigger problems.

Proofreading Marks	
∧	Add
⊙	Period
ℒ	Take out
≡	Capital letter
/	Small letter

 Did you correct six pronouns that were used incorrectly?

WRITE

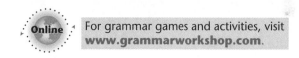

You can combine sentences that have subject pronouns.
Use a plural subject pronoun to replace the singular pronouns,
or join the pronouns with *and*. Use a plural verb in the
combined sentence.

She enjoys science fiction.	We enjoy science fiction.
I enjoy science fiction.	She **and** I enjoy science fiction.

You can also combine sentences that have object pronouns that
share the same action. Replace the singular pronouns with a
plural pronoun, or join the pronouns with *and*.

Max gave her a book.	Max gave them a book.
Max gave him a book.	Max gave her **and** him a book.

Anna waved to him.	Anna waved to us.
Anna waved to me.	Anna waved to him **and** me.

D *Combine each pair of sentences. You can either use a plural pronoun
or join the pronouns with the word **and**. The first one is done for you.*

1. He read *Treasure Island*. I read *Treasure Island*.

We read Treasure Island.

2. Mr. Gomez gave him *Helen Keller: Rebellious Spirit*. Mr. Gomez gave me
Helen Keller: Rebellious Spirit.

3. Read the book to him. Read the book to her.

4. The librarian reads to you. The librarian reads to him.

5. Please give some books to him. Please give some books to me.

Lesson 39: **Using *I* and *Me*, *We* and *Us***

LEARN

■ The pronoun *I* is a subject pronoun. Use *I* as the subject of a sentence.

Last month, **I** started to collect stamps.

■ The pronoun *me* is an object pronoun. Use *me* as a direct object or as the object of a preposition.

DIRECT OBJECT   Rita gave **me** a stamp album.
OBJECT OF PREPOSITION   She gave some stamps to **me**.

■ When you speak or write about yourself and another person, always name the other person first. Use the rules above to help you decide which pronoun to use.

Last week, **my brother and I** traded stamps for the first time.
Yesterday, Richard traded stamps with **my brother and me**.

Richard and I joined a stamp club earlier today.
Mr. Block showed his collection to **Richard and me**.

■ Sometimes a noun is used with *we* or *us* to make it clear whom you are talking about.

• Use *we* with noun subjects.
We newcomers to the club were amazed at all the different kinds of stamps.

• Use *us* with a direct object or the object of a preposition.
These stamps belong to **us club members**.

PRACTICE

A *Write the pronoun in parentheses that correctly completes each sentence.*

1. _____ like American stamps best. (I, me)

2. The colors and designs of these stamps fascinate _____. (I, me)

3. A stamp catalog tells _____ collectors about the value of each stamp. (we, us)

4. _____ Americans issued our first stamps in 1847. (We, Us)

5. Katie and _____ have seen some of the first U.S. stamps. (I, me)

6. My aunt gave Katie and _____ some letters with old stamps on them. (I, me)

7. Last year, _____ bought an old stamp album at a yard sale. (I, me)

8. Studying stamps has taught Katie and _____ about U.S. history. (I, me)

9. _____ stamp collectors also collect stamps from other countries. (We, Us)

10. Those stamps teach _____ about world geography. (we, us)

B *Write the word or words in parentheses that correctly complete each sentence.*

1. My sister Anna and _____ collect coins. (I, me)

2. Two years ago, my grandfather gave _____ some old silver dollars. (I, me)

3. _____ have been collecting coins ever since. (We, Us)

4. _____ both collect Lincoln pennies. (Anna and me, Anna and I)

5. Together, _____ sisters have almost every penny minted after 1912. (we, us)

6. My sister and _____ look for coins in very good condition. (I, me)

7. The state quarters fascinate Anna and _____, too. (I, me)

8. Each year, the government makes new state designs for _____ collectors. (we, us)

9. Last fall, _____ dug up an 1888 penny in our garden. (I and Anna, Anna and I)

10. _____ like this penny best even though it is in poor condition. (Anna and I, Anna and me)

C Anna wrote this thank-you note to another coin collector in her town. She made eight mistakes when using the pronouns *I* and *me*, and *we* and *us*. Use the proofreading marks in the box to correct her mistakes.

Dear Mrs. Flynn,

My classmates and me want to thank you for coming to our coin club. Your valuable coins impressed we coin collectors. My sister and I liked your silver dollars. Us have a few silver dollars, too.

Your talk helped the other class members and we sisters to know the difference between "very good" condition and "fine" condition. Now my sister and me can grade coins.

Thank you for leaving the old coin catalogs for our friends and we. Us sisters plan to visit the collection at the State Museum. We club members will go as a group.

Thanks again,

Anna Davis

P.S. me just found a 1918D Lincoln penny in some change. It's in very good condition!

Proofreading Marks

∧	Add
⊙	Period
ℒ	Take out
≡	Capital letter
/	Small letter

  Did you correct eight mistakes with the pronouns *I*, *me*, *we*, and *us*?

WRITE

D *Write a sentence using the words in parentheses. Write about a hobby or something special that you enjoy doing.*

1. (us fifth graders) _____

_____

2. (we fifth graders) _____

_____

3. (my best friend and me) _____

_____

4. (my best friends and I) _____

_____

5. (my family and I) _____

_____

6. (my family and me) _____

_____

7. (my cousins and us) _____

_____

8. (our relatives and we) _____

_____

Proofreading Checklist ✓

❏ *Did you use subject pronouns as the subjects of your sentences?*

❏ *Did you use object pronouns as direct objects or objects of prepositions?*

Lesson 40: Possessive and Demonstrative Pronouns

LEARN

■ A **possessive pronoun** takes the place of a possessive noun. It shows *who* or *what* has or owns something.

> **John's** class planned a yard sale. (possessive noun)
> **His** class planned a yard sale. (possessive pronoun)

There are two kinds of possessive pronouns. The possessive pronouns *my, your, his, her, its, our,* and *their* appear before a noun. The possessive pronouns *mine, yours, his, hers, its, ours,* and *theirs* stand alone.

Before a Noun	Stand Alone
My old bike is in good shape.	This kite is **mine**.
We can sell it at **our** yard sale.	**Ours** are on the table.
Jenna sold **her** old scooter.	The skates are **hers**, too.
Your tennis racket sold quickly.	**Yours** are right here.
Where is **their** basketball?	The football is **theirs**.

■ The **demonstrative pronouns** *this, that, these,* and *those* point out a specific person, place, or thing. Use *this* and *these* to point out things that are nearby. Use *that* and *those* to point out things that are farther away.

Nearby	Farther Away
This is a big sale!	**That** costs a dollar.
Do **these** still work?	Eric bought **those** over there.

Do not use *here* or *there* with demonstrative pronouns.

INCORRECT	Have you ever seen **that there** before?
CORRECT	Have you ever seen **that** before?

PRACTICE

Read each sentence. Underline each possessive pronoun. Circle each demonstrative pronoun. Write the pronoun on the line.

1. Here are your old comic books. _____

2. Mine are still in Dad's car. _____

3. Does the blue jacket fit my brother? _____

4. Do the puzzles have all their pieces? _____

5. Should we lower our prices for them? _____

6. This is a fund-raiser for the playground. _____

7. Do you want to buy those, too? _____

8. These go well with the shoes. _____

9. Are those for sale at the same price? _____

10. I cannot understand that. _____

B *Write the possessive or demonstrative pronoun in parentheses that correctly completes each sentence.*

1. _____ plan is to raise $500 for the playground. (Our, Ours)

2. Will _____ be enough money to build it? (that, those)

3. No, but other classes will have _____ fund-raisers later. (their, theirs)

4. Mr. Ames cleaned out _____ garage for the sale. (its, his)

5. My grandmother cleaned out _____, too! (her, hers)

6. Are _____ your old baseball cards in front of me? (these, those)

7. No, _____ sold during the first minutes of the sale. (my, mine)

8. Did the Catnap Bookshop contribute _____ old books? (it, its)

9. _____ on the table over there came from the shop. (These, Those)

10. _____ sale is going to be a big success! (Our, Ours)

C Len wrote this personal narrative about the class yard sale. He made eight mistakes in the use of possessive pronouns and demonstrative pronouns. Use the proofreading marks in the box to correct the mistakes.

Proofreading Marks

∧ Add
⊙ Period
ℒ Take out
≡ Capital letter
/ Small letter

When our class was having its yard sale, Mom gave me this here to sell. The old floor lamp had been in our attic for years. I would have put it in mine room, but our class needed things for the sale.

A woman bought the lamp right away. The problem was hers car. The lamp was too tall for the tiny car. "These won't fit in my car," the woman explained, handing back the lamp to me. "But keep the money," she added. "I want you kids to have yours playground."

The lamp was our to sell again. Around three o'clock, two women could not decide whether they wanted to buy the lamp. In the end, they bought it.

After the sale was over, I walked home and spotted our old lamp in a trash can. The lamp was my again!

"I told you to sell those," Mom said when she saw the old lamp.

"I did sell it," I replied. "Twice!"

Did you correct eight possessive pronouns and demonstrative pronouns?

WRITE

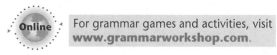

Online · For grammar games and activities, visit **www.grammarworkshop.com**.

D *Have you ever bought or sold anything at a yard sale, garage sale, or flea market? Have you ever traded baseball cards, comics, or DVDs with a friend or sibling? Write about your experience, or use your imagination if you haven't had this experience. Describe the objects, and tell why you bought, sold, or traded them. Use at least four possessive pronouns and one demonstrative pronoun in your sentences.*

_____

_____

_____

_____

_____

_____

_____

_____

_____

_____

_____

_____

_____

Proofreading Checklist ✓

❑ *Did you use at least four possessive pronouns and one demonstrative pronoun in your sentences?*

Lesson 41: **Pronouns and Antecedents**

LEARN

- A **pronoun** is a word that takes the place of a noun. The pronoun's **antecedent** is the noun the pronoun refers to. In each of the sentences below, the noun in boldface is the antecedent of the pronoun in boldface.

    Maria read three fairy tales. **She** read them in the library. The **tales** were so beautiful that Maria remembered **them**. **Jack** enjoys fairy tales, and **his** friends do, too.

- A pronoun must agree with its antecedent in number. This means that if the noun is singular, the pronoun must also be singular. If the noun is plural, the pronoun must also be plural.

In the first sentence above, the singular pronoun *she* refers to the singular noun *Maria*. In the second sentence, *them* refers to the plural noun *tales*. In the third sentence, *his* refers to the singular noun *Jack*.

PRACTICE

A *Underline the pronoun in each sentence. Write the noun that is its antecedent. The first one is done for you.*

1. Beauty must save her father's life. _____Beauty_____

2. The castle is far away, and it looks dark and threatening. _____

3. The owner looks like a monster, but he is kind. _____

4. The Beast likes Beauty and gives her many gifts. _____

5. Beauty returns home with the gifts and shows them to the villagers. _____

6. The Beast becomes very ill when his young guest leaves. _____

7. When Beauty returns, she finds the Beast close to death. _____

8. Finally, Beauty realizes that she loves the Beast. _____

9. Both characters declare their love for each other. _____

10. Readers are happy when they read the story's ending. _____

B *Write the pronoun in parentheses that correctly completes each sentence.*

1. A husband and wife live alone in a tiny hut. _____ are poor and hungry. (They, She)

2. Outside, a cold wind blows hard. _____ shakes the tiny house. (They, It)

3. A beautiful lady appears, and _____ gives the couple three wishes. (she, it)

4. The lady promises the wishes will come true and warns the couple to

use _____ carefully. (it, them)

5. The husband and wife cannot believe _____ good luck! (their, its)

6. The man and woman agree that _____ must not waste the three wishes. (they, we)

7. The wife makes _____ first wish without thinking. (his, her)

8. The husband is surprised when _____ sees a sausage on the table. (I, he)

9. The man becomes angry with his wife and wishes the sausage was

attached to _____ nose. (her, its)

10. The husband has used _____ wish foolishly, too! (its, his)

11. The husband and wife use _____ third wish to remove the sausage from the woman's nose. (our, their)

12. The man and woman realize that _____ have wasted all three wishes. (they, we)

C *Elise wrote this summary of a Japanese fairy tale, "The Magic Mortar." She made seven mistakes when using pronouns. Use the proofreading marks in the box to correct the mistakes.*

A poor man had almost no food for their wife and children. He went to his rich brother to ask for a loan, but the greedy brother would not give him anything. Empty-handed, the disappointed peasant walked home. Along the way, he worried about his wife and children. What would he tell her?

On the road, the peasant met an old woman. "Have you any food for me?" the woman asked. The peasant smiled at the old woman and handed it a small rice cake. It was the only food that his own wife had given he when he set out that morning.

The old woman took the little rice cake and hungrily ate them. "You're very generous," she said. To reward the peasant for your generosity, she handed him a mortar, or rice grinder.

At home, the peasant put the mortar on the floor and turned its handle. A steady supply of fine rice streamed out of the magic mortar. The peasant and his family could not believe its good fortune. For years and years, the magic mortar continued to feed the family well.

Proofreading Marks

∧	Add
⊙	Period
ℓ	Take out
≡	Capital letter
/	Small letter

Did you find and correct seven pronouns?

WRITE

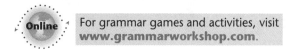
D Write a short summary of one of your favorite fairy tales. You could summarize "Cinderella" or "Snow White," for example. Include at least five pronouns in your sentences. Make sure that the pronouns agree with their antecedents.

Proofreading Checklist ✓

❏ *Does each pronoun agree with its antecedent?*

Lesson 42: **Contractions with Pronouns**

LEARN

■ A **contraction** is a shortened word made by combining
two words. An apostrophe (') takes the place of any
letters that are left out.
Many contractions are formed by combining a pronoun
and a verb.

Pronoun and Verb	Contraction	Pronoun and Verb	Contraction
I am	**I'm**	I have	**I've**
she is	**she's**	she has	**she's**
it is	**it's**	it has	**it's**
you are	**you're**	you have	**you've**
they are	**they're**	they have	**they've**
I will	**I'll**	I had	**I'd**
you will	**you'll**	you had	**you'd**
we would	**we'd**	we had	**we'd**

■ Notice that the contractions for the pronouns with the verbs *is*
and *has* are the same. The contractions for the pronouns with
the verbs *would* and *had* are also the same.

She's late. (is)	**We'd** better hurry. (had)
She's lost track of time. (has)	**We'd** catch the next bus. (would)

PRACTICE

*Write the words that make up each contraction. (Some contractions
stand for more than one pronoun and verb.)*

1. they'd _____

2. we've _____

3. I've _____

4. she'll _____

5. he'd _____

6. it's _____

7. they'll _____

8. we've _____

9. you'd _____

10. I'm _____

B *Read each saying. Write a contraction for the pronoun and verb in **boldface**.*

1. **We have** nothing to fear but fear itself. _____

2. They say that **it is** never too late to change. _____

3. **We will** never forget what's-his-name. _____

4. **We are** most likely to remember what we most want to forget. _____

5. I think that **I am** sitting on top of the world! _____

6. **You are** born with your relatives, but you pick your friends. _____

7. Every book is new until **you have** read it. _____

8. **I would** rather be right than be president. _____

9. **They are** either part of the solution or part of the problem. _____

10. **I have** never met a person I didn't like. _____

11. Unfortunately, **he is** all talk and no action. _____

12. If their faces looked funny, **they would** blame the mirror. _____

13. **It is** always morning somewhere in the world. _____

14. **I would** be more careful next time. _____

15. **They had** seen it all before. _____

C *Jason wrote a short essay about everyday expressions. In these paragraphs from his essay, Jason spelled eight contractions incorrectly. Use the proofreading marks in the box to correct the mistakes.*

Remember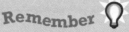
An apostrophe (') takes the place of any letters that are left out in a contraction.

There are some everyday sayings that Il'l never understand. Take the expression, "You are what you eat." Mom says that one all the time. Shes most likely to say it when I'm trying to avoid the spinach. "Mom!" I tell her. "If you're what you eat, I'm not eating this spinach! Id rather not be all mushy and green!"

Another saying is "You're as young as you feel." Youve probably heard it, too. My grandfather says that one. He'll be 65 years old in June, and hes in great shape. He says he feels as if he is 21. Maybe hed like to be 21 again, but he isn't really. Yes, he can throw a baseball farther than I can, but I can usually beat him in a bicycle race.

"It's a small world after all!" That is another saying that annoys me. People often say it when theyve run into someone they know. In reality, the world is large. Its hard to imagine anything larger. Also, the number of people is rising at a rapid rate. It's really a bigger world after all!

Proofreading Marks

∧	Add
⊙	Period
ℓ	Take out
≡	Capital letter
/	Small letter

Did you fix eight contractions that were spelled incorrectly?

WRITE

Online — For grammar games and activities, visit **www.grammarworkshop.com**.

D *Write about some of the things you and your friends and family enjoy doing on weekends. In each sentence, include the contraction for the words in parentheses.*

1. (I have)

_____

2. (I am)

_____

3. (she will)

_____

4. (she has)

_____

5. (they would)

_____

6. (he had)

_____

7. (you will)

_____

8. (he is)

_____

9. (you are)

_____

Proofreading Checklist ☑

❏ *Did you write each pronoun and verb as a contraction?*
❏ *Did you spell each contraction correctly?*

Lesson 43: Using Homophones

LEARN

■ **Homophones** are words that sound alike but have different spellings and different meanings. Do not confuse the possessive pronouns *its, your,* and *their* with the homophones *it's, you're, they're,* and *there.*

Homophone	Meaning	Sentence
it's	*it is* or *it has*	**It's** the best joke book.
its	belonging to *it*	**Its** jokes are so funny.
you're	*you are*	**You're** my favorite joke teller.
your	belonging to *you*	**Your** jokes are funny.
they're	*they are*	**They're** ready to hear some riddles.
their	belonging to *them*	**Their** riddles are easy.
there	in that place	**There** are more riddles here.

The contraction *they're* has two homophones. One is the possessive pronoun *their*, and the other one is the adverb *there*.

■ **When you write, use the correct homophone. Think about the meaning and spelling of the word you want.**

Do not confuse possessive pronouns with contractions. Remember that possessive pronouns do not have apostrophes.

POSSESSIVE PRONOUN	You and **your** friend tell funny jokes.
CONTRACTION	**You're** early for the joke-telling contest.

PRACTICE

A *Read each group of words. If the homophone is used correctly, write **correct**. If it is not used correctly, write the correct homophone.*

1. there silly jokes ——————

2. your muddy shoes ——————

3. its tricky ——————

4. right over there ——————

5. its constant hum ——————

6. you're winning smile ——————

7. their laughter ——————

8. your recent letter ——————

9. wag it's tail ——————

10. give they're approval ——————

B *Write the word in parentheses that correctly completes each sentence.*

1. What goes up and down in _____ body without moving? (your, you're)

2. _____ is no such thing in my body. (Their, There)

3. Yes, _____ your temperature! (its, it's)

4. _____ first and last letters are *e*, but this has only one letter in it. (Its, It's)

5. _____ making this up, aren't you? (You're, Your)

6. No, _____ the word *envelope*! (its, it's)

7. Why are so many students turning in _____ math books? (their, there)

8. _____ finding too many problems in those books! (They're, There)

9. Did you know that a word is spelled incorrectly in _____ dictionary? (you're, your)

10. Yes, _____ the word *incorrectly*. (its, it's)

11. Why do Monarch butterflies fly south to _____ winter home in Mexico? (their, there)

12. _____ much too far to walk! (Its, It's)

13. What has no beginning, no end, and nothing in _____ middle? (its, it's)

14. It's that donut _____ eating. (your, you're)

C *Denise wrote a script for a comedy act for her school's talent show. In her script, she used ten homophones incorrectly. Use the proofreading marks in the box to correct her mistakes.*

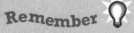

Remember

Think about the meanings and the spellings of the homophones you use.

How many of you hate elephant jokes? They're the least funny jokes in the whole world! If your lucky enough not to know any, let me ruin you're day.

Q: How do you know if an elephant has been in your refrigerator?

A: You can see it's footprints in the butter.

Even though your laughing, their is nothing funny about that joke. Like all elephant jokes, its just silly and illogical. Let's try another one.

Q: How do you know when their are two elephants in your refrigerator?

A: Your unable to close the refrigerator door.

If you're like most people, you didn't even try to guess the answers. There is absolutely no way to figure them out. They make no sense. Here is another elephant joke for you listeners out they're.

Q: What's the difference between an elephant and a plum?

A: Its obvious. An elephant is gray.

Proofreading Marks

∧	Add
⊙	Period
ℰ	Take out
≡	Capital letter
/	Small letter

 Did you correct ten mistakes with homophones?

Write Your Own

WRITE

D On the lines below, make up an answer for each elephant
joke. Your answer can be silly, ridiculous, or totally illogical.
In each answer, use one of the homophones on page 192.

1. Q: How do you know if there are three elephants in your refrigerator?

A: _____

_____

2. Q: What is the difference between an elephant and a bunch of bananas?

A: _____

_____

3. Q: Why do elephants paint their toenails red?

A: _____

_____

4. Q: Why aren't there any elephants in fifth grade?

A: _____

_____

5. Q: How do you know if there is an elephant under the bed?

A: _____

_____

6. Q: Why does the elephant cross the road on Saturdays?

A: _____

_____

Proofreading Checklist ✓

❑ *Did you use **its**, **it's**, **your**, **you're**, **there**, **they're**, and **their**
correctly?*

Subject Pronouns (pp. 168–171) *Underline the subject pronoun in each sentence. Then write the present-tense form of the verb in parentheses that agrees with the subject pronoun.*

1. I (build) a snow fort after the snowstorm.   _____

2. It (stretch) for several feet.   _____

3. They (offer) to help with the fort.   _____

4. He (carry) the blocks of snow to the other end.   _____

Object Pronouns (pp. 172–175) *Underline the object pronoun in each sentence.*

5. David saw me working on the snow fort.

6. We showed them how we formed the window.

7. You helped David build it.

8. I watched him from the snow fort.

Using *I* and *Me*, *We* and *Us* (pp. 176–179) *Underline the pronoun in parentheses that correctly completes each sentence.*

9. David told Philip and (I, me) that we should name our snow fort.

10. Lisa told (we, us) that her fort's name was Fort Washington.

11. (We, Us) decided on the next best name.

12. Fort Jefferson sounded good to Philip and (I, me).

Possessive and Demonstrative Pronouns (pp. 180–183)
Find the possessive pronoun or demonstrative pronoun in each sentence. Underline each possessive pronoun. Circle each demonstrative pronoun.

13. Our snow forts were finished after an hour.

14. We had a big fort, but theirs was bigger.

15. "These will be great for a snowball fight," David said.

16. This was a fun afternoon.

Pronouns and Antecedents (pp. 184–187) *Underline the noun that is the antecedent of the pronoun in* **boldface**.

17. Lena said that **she** had a better idea.

18. The forts are beautiful, and a snowball fight might ruin **them**.

19. The others said that **they** agreed with Lena.

20. We built a snow bridge, and **it** lasted until April.

Contractions with Pronouns (pp. 188–191) *Read each sentence. Write a contraction for the pronoun and verb in* **boldface**.

21. She has been a big help to us.   _____

22. They have been asking about you.   _____

23. We are ready to go inside.   _____

24. David says that **he is** frozen.   _____

Using Homophones (pp. 192–195) *Underline the homophone in parentheses that correctly completes each sentence.*

25. (Its, It's) much colder today than it was yesterday.

26. Are you sure (you're, your) not too cold?

27. They decided to improve (they're, their) fort.

28. They built a snowman over (there, their).

DIRECTIONS *Fill in the circle next to the sentence that spells and uses pronouns, verbs, contractions, and homophones correctly.*

1. ○ Me and my cousin are at the train station with Grandma.

   ○ She take the train fairly often.

   ○ Its the first train trip for Denny and me.

   ○ We're excited about our trip.

2. ○ Denny and I walk around the station.

   ○ A loud voice announces times over their.

   ○ It announce our train.

   ○ Our is on Track 12.

3. ○ We walks down to Track 12.

   ○ We're amazed by the train's engine.

   ○ That there is huge!

   ○ It's job is to pull 20 cars.

4. ○ The engineer waves to Denny and I.

   ○ He's standing by the engine.

   ○ A man helps we and Grandma.

   ○ He carrys our suitcases to the train.

5. ○ Grandma shows us to our seats.

   ○ There really comfortable!

   ○ We hands our tickets to the conductor.

   ○ Hes moving up the aisle.

6. ○ The train starts and surprises us.

   ○ It lurchs away from the station.

   ○ It pick up speed outside the city.

   ○ Soon wer'e going 90 miles an hour!

7. ○ I watch the countryside as they roll by.

   ○ The fields out their are so green!

   ○ It's more fun than a plane ride.

   ○ Your able to see more from a train.

8. ○ This here is the dining car.

   ○ Weve walked through five cars.

   ○ Grandma orders food for Denny and I.

   ○ It's very tasty.

9. ○ You're bed on a train isn't very big.

   ○ Your comfortable enough to sleep.

   ○ I see lights, and there flashing past.

   ○ I'm rocking to the train's rhythm.

10. ○ We moves quickly over the tracks.

    ○ The train speeds up, and then he slows down.

    ○ Im not sure when I fell asleep.

    ○ I didn't wake up until we'd arrived.

DIRECTIONS *Read the paragraphs, and look carefully at each underlined part. Fill in the circle next to the answer choice that shows the correct use and spelling of pronouns, verbs, contractions, and homophones. If the underlined part is already correct, fill in the circle for "Correct as is."*

If your like most of we Americans, you probably haven't taken a train
    (11)
lately. Well, you'll be glad to hear their are benefits to traveling by train. For
           (12)
one thing, trains cause less pollution than cars and planes. Windy conditions

do not make their rides bumpy, and it's impossible to get jet lag on a train.
          (13)
Unfortunately, most trains are a lot slower than planes. However,

those there trains running between Washington and Boston reach speeds of
    (14)
150 miles per hour. My father and me have made better time on them than on
         (15)
airplanes. Best of all, trains are relaxing. You can watch the scenery, take a stroll,

and order a meal. Trains are terrific! For good transportation, you can't beat it.
           (16)

11. ○ your like most of us
   ○ you're like most of we
   ○ you're like most of us
   ○ Correct as is

12. ○ you'll be glad to hear they're
   ○ youl'l be glad to hear their
   ○ you'll be glad to hear there
   ○ Correct as is

13. ○ they're rides bumpy, and its
   ○ there rides bumpy, and its
   ○ their rides bumpy, and its
   ○ Correct as is

14. ○ this here trains
   ○ these here trains
   ○ those trains
   ○ Correct as is

15. ○ Me and my father
   ○ My father and I
   ○ I and my father
   ○ Correct as is

16. ○ they
   ○ them
   ○ these
   ○ Correct as is

Lesson 44: **Writing Sentences Correctly**

LEARN

■ **When you write, begin every sentence with a capital letter. End every sentence with an end punctuation mark.**

   Have you studied ancient Egypt**?** **T**hat society fascinates me.

■ **The end punctuation mark you use depends on the kind of sentence you write.**

Pyramids of Giza, Egypt

• **End a declarative sentence with a period (.).**
   The history of Egypt goes back 5000 years**.**

• **End an interrogative sentence with a question mark (?).**
   How old are the pyramids**?**

• **End an exclamatory sentence with an exclamation mark (!).**
   What a long history Egypt has**!**

• **End an imperative sentence with a period (.).**
   Read this book about ancient Egypt**.**

PRACTICE

A *Read each item. Write **correct** or **incorrect** to tell whether the sentence or sentences are written correctly.*

1. The pharaohs ruled Egypt have you read about them. _____

2. Look at these models of the pyramids. _____

3. Were the pyramids built as tombs for the pharaohs. _____

4. How huge this pyramid is it is the Great Pyramid? _____

5. Wow, it is the largest stone building on Earth? _____

6. Is it really solid stone with just a few passageways? _____

7. Let me see those pictures what kind of writing is that. _____

8. Egyptian writing is called hieroglyphics. _____

9. The Egyptians had many gods these temples honored them. _____

10. What interests you most about ancient Egypt! _____

B *Write these sentences correctly. Use capital letters and the correct end punctuation marks.*

1. we saw the Egyptian exhibit at the museum did you see it _____

_____

2. the exhibit includes part of a tomb it's very beautiful _____

_____

3. three mummies are also in the exhibit _____

_____

4. mummies were wrapped in cloth then they were put in coffins _____

_____

5. wow, some of these mummies are more than 3000 years old _____

_____

6. does the exhibit include any ancient sculptures _____

_____

7. sculptors carved huge statues of the pharaohs and gods _____

_____

8. are those carvings called sphinxes _____

_____

9. go see the traveling exhibit before it closes _____

_____

Peter wrote this report about the scribes of ancient Egypt. He made two mistakes in the use of capitalization and seven mistakes in the use of end punctuation in the sentences. Use the proofreading marks to correct the errors.

Most Egyptian children did not go to school boys went to work at an early age. Girls stayed at home and learned household skills. The boys who did go to school were taught hieroglyphics and usually became scribes?

In hieroglyphics, each symbol stands for an object or a sound. Can you remember having to learn the 26 letters of the alphabet. Egyptian boys had to learn more than 800 hieroglyphs. What a hard job that must have been.

Young scribes practiced writing on boards and broken pots. Only later did they use papyrus, which came from a Nile River plant. Did you know that our word *paper* comes from the Egyptian word *papyrus.*

Scribes became teachers, librarians, and government officials. Some scribes produced works of literature some works have survived. How fortunate we are to have them.

Did you correct two mistakes with capitalization and seven mistakes with end punctuation?

WRITE

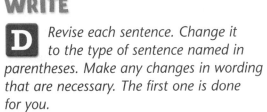

D *Revise each sentence. Change it to the type of sentence named in parentheses. Make any changes in wording that are necessary. The first one is done for you.*

Online — For grammar games and activities, visit **www.grammarworkshop.com**.

1. Why was the Nile River important in ancient Egypt? (declarative)

The Nile River was important in ancient Egypt.

2. If you look at this map, you will see why. (imperative)

3. Much of Egypt was a lifeless desert. (interrogative)

4. All the green areas are along the Nile River. (interrogative)

5. Will you tell me where most ancient Egyptians lived? (imperative)

6. They lived and farmed along the banks of the Nile. (interrogative)

7. Was the soil rich and fertile because of the floods? (declarative)

8. Can you trace the Nile from central Africa to the Mediterranean Sea? (imperative)

9. The Nile flows for 4100 miles. (exclamatory)

Lesson 45: Capitalizing Proper Nouns and Adjectives

LEARN

■ A **proper noun** names a specific person, place, or thing. Capitalize all the important words in a proper noun.

Chinese lion dancer

- Capitalize the names of people and special groups.
  Amy Jones   Boy Scouts   New York Yankees

- The names of special places begin with a capital letter.
  Washington, D.C.   Gulf of Mexico
  Kings County   Park Avenue
  John Hancock Tower   Times Square

- Capitalize the names of days, months, and holidays.
  Tuesday   June   Fourth of July

- Capitalize family titles that refer to specific people only when they are used before a name or as a name.
  Uncle Joe took us to the Museum of Modern Art.
  My uncle enjoys visiting art museums.

- Capitalize titles of respect that are used before a name.
  President Lincoln   Senator John Glenn

■ Capitalize **proper adjectives** formed from proper nouns. If a proper adjective is two words, capitalize both words.
  China   Chinese lion dances
  South America   South American music

PRACTICE

A *In the sentences, underline the nouns and adjectives that should begin with a capital letter.*

1. Last week, aunt em and I went to the empire state building.

2. It was part of a trip that we girl scouts took to new york city.

3. We went there on a holiday, labor day, so it was crowded.

4. We shared our elevator with a group of brazilian schoolchildren.

5. This skyscraper was built by william durant.

6. The building was officially opened by president herbert hoover on May 1, 1931.

7. When it was built, this building was the tallest american skyscraper.

8. Today, the sears tower in chicago is taller than this structure.

9. The observation deck on the 102nd floor has a fine view of the hudson river.

10. My aunt used to live across the harlem river in manhattan.

B *Rewrite each sentence. Capitalize each proper noun or proper adjective correctly.*

1. During our trip, we met Grandma jones at herald square. _____

2. We traveled by subway to central park. _____

3. We saw the statue of duke ellington at 110th street and fifth avenue. _____

4. The jacqueline kennedy onassis reservoir shone in the sunlight. _____

5. I liked cleopatra's needle, an ancient egyptian obelisk, or tower. _____

6. We played near the statue of balto, a famous sled dog. _____

7. This siberian husky carried medicine to nome, alaska. _____

C Read this part of Janna's report about the United Nations. In all, Janna made ten mistakes. She capitalized four words that should be lowercase, and she didn't capitalize six proper nouns. Use the proofreading marks in the box to correct these mistakes.

Proofreading Marks

∧	Add
⊙	Period
ℓ	Take out
≡	Capital letter
/	Small letter

On august 21, 1944, representatives from the United States, the Soviet Union, the united kingdom, and China met at Dumbarton Oaks in Washington, D.C. They started a new Organization for world peace. A year later, delegates from 46 Nations met in San Francisco to write a charter for the United Nations.

The United Nations (or UN) is on 18 acres in New York City along the east river. The flags of 192 member countries fly on first avenue from 42nd Street to 48th Street. When you enter the UN gates, you are actually leaving new york city. The land and buildings of the UN are owned by its member nations.

UN delegates from 192 countries meet to discuss world issues. The UN symbol hangs above the delegates. The symbol is a map of the World as seen from the north pole. Around the map are olive branches, which are symbols of Peace.

Look Back
Did you capitalize six proper nouns?
Did you lowercase four common nouns that begin with a capital letter?

WRITE

D *Think about a well-known place that you have visited recently or a place that you would like to visit someday. On the lines below, write five or more sentences about the place. Tell why it is special, what you liked most about it, or why you want to visit it. In your sentences, use a mix of proper nouns and proper adjectives. You should use at least five altogether.*

Ellis Island Immigration Museum

_____

_____

_____

_____

_____

_____

_____

_____

_____

_____

_____

_____

_____

Proofreading Checklist ☑

❏ *Did you use at least five proper nouns and proper adjectives altogether in your sentences?*
❏ *Did you capitalize each proper noun and proper adjective?*

Lesson 46: **Abbreviations**

LEARN

■ An **abbreviation** is a short form of a word that begins with a capital letter and ends with a period. Use most abbreviations only in special kinds of writing, such as addresses.

Titles of Respect

Mr. Lee Figueroa   **Ms.** Ann Chen   **Dr.** Marian Spragg

Businesses

The Closet **Co.**   Hamilton **Corp.**

Addresses

St. (Street)   **Rd.** (Road)   **P.O.** (Post Office)
Ave. (Avenue)   **Blvd.** (Boulevard)   **Rte.** (Route)

Months and Days of the Week

Jan. Feb. Mar. Apr. Aug. Sept. Oct. Nov. Dec.
Sun. Mon. Tues. Wed. Thurs. Fri. Sat.

■ An **initial** is an abbreviation of a first or middle name. An initial is written as a capital letter followed by a period.

Eric Paul Mori   **E. P.** Mori   Rae Ann Lee   Rae **A.** Lee

■ State names used with ZIP codes have two-letter abbreviations. Capitalize both letters, but don't use periods.

FL (Florida)   **GA** (Georgia)   **SC** (South Carolina)

PRACTICE

 Write each name or abbreviation correctly.

1. Fairmont ave _____

2. Dr Vivian b Jain _____

3. mr Tom a Chase _____

4. 117 Salisbury rd _____

5. Feb 11, 2008 _____

6. Sunshine Garden co _____

7. j. s. Howe _____

8. po Box 111 _____

9. Naples, Fl 34104 _____

10. Milford corp _____

B *Follow the directions in parentheses to change each item. Write the item using capital letters and periods correctly. The first one is done for you.*

1. Barbara Ann Miller

   <u>   B. A. Miller   </u>
   (Use two initials.)

2. 88 Kings Boulevard

   _____
   (Use an abbreviation.)

3. Doctor Emerson Graye

   _____
   (Use an abbreviation.)

4. Open Sunday–Thursday, 8–4

   _____
   (Use two abbreviations.)

5. August 17, 2008

   _____
   (Use an abbreviation.)

6. Mister Alan Mason Lee

   _____
   (Use an initial and an abbreviation.)

7. 27565 Route 23

   _____
   (Use an abbreviation.)

8. Julia Hernandez Corporation

   _____
   (Use an initial and an abbreviation.)

9. Post Office Box 124

   _____
   (Use an abbreviation.)

10. Ms. Jane Anna Garone

    _____
    (Use two initials.)

11. Charleston, South Carolina 29401

    _____
    (Use an abbreviation.)

12. Monday, August 28–Friday, September 29

    _____
    (Use four abbreviations.)

C *In the items below, ten of the abbreviations are written incorrectly. Use the proofreading marks in the box to correct the errors.*

Remember

Most abbreviations begin with a capital letter and end with a period.

1.

John a Peters
28 Preston blvd
Orlando, FL 32804

R Davis Publishing Corp
P.O. Box 211
Atlanta, Ga 30303

Proofreading Marks

∧	Add
⊙	Period
ℓ	Take out
≡	Capital letter
/	Small letter

2.

Come to the Track Team Annual Car Wash!

Place:

Sanders Elementary School
Corner of Marigold rd and Mayfair st

Day/Date:

Sat. – Mar 25, 2008

Time:

9–4

3.

Date   Oct. 8

For   Tyra

Quality Photo co   called.

Message   Your photos are

ready for pickup. The store is

open fri and Sat. until 6 o'clock.

Did you correct ten errors with abbreviations?

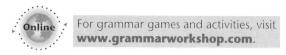
WRITE

D *Imagine that you took each telephone message below for members of your family. Fill in the message pad with the missing information. Use correct abbreviations whenever possible.*

1. Doctor Lopez's office called your sister Ellen on January 20. The office was able to change Ellen's appointment from January 28 to February 6 at 11 o'clock.

Date _____

For _____

_____ called.

Message _____

_____

_____

2. Mister Graye from Ace Auto Company called on March 26. He has a car that your father might want to buy. The company's new auto showroom at 1080 Kennedy Boulevard is open from Monday to Saturday, from 9 to 9.

Date _____

For _____

_____ called.

Message _____

_____

_____

Proofreading Checklist ✔

❑ *Did you capitalize and use a period with each initial?*
❑ *Did you capitalize and use a period with each abbreviation?*

Lesson 47: **Titles**

LEARN

The titles of written works are set off in special ways.

- Titles of books, magazines, movies, and newspapers are set off by italics in printed material. When you write by hand, underline these titles.

PRINTED	*The Chicago Tribune* (newspaper)
HANDWRITTEN	<u>The Chicago Tribune</u>

PRINTED	*Ranger Rick* (magazine)
HANDWRITTEN	<u>Ranger Rick</u>

- Titles of short stories, book chapters, articles, songs, and most poems are set off by quotation marks.

    "Aladdin and the Magic Lamp" (short story)
    "What I Heard in the Apple Barrel" (book chapter)
    "Exploring a Coral Reef" (magazine article)
    "The Rain in Spain" (song)
    "The Walrus and the Carpenter" (poem)

- Notice that the first word and each important word in the titles begin with a capital letter. Words such as *a, an, and, as, at, for, in, of, the,* and *to* are not capitalized unless they are the first or last word in the title.

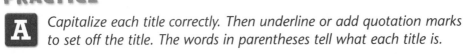

PRACTICE

A *Capitalize each title correctly. Then underline or add quotation marks to set off the title. The words in parentheses tell what each title is.*

1. around the world in eighty days (book) _____

2. cricket (magazine) _____

3. expectations (magazine article) _____

4. casey at the bat (poem) _____

5. the circus comes to town (book chapter) _____

6. harry potter and the sorcerer's stone (book) _____

7. down in the valley (song) _____

8. the legend of sleepy hollow (short story) _____

9. national geographic kids (magazine) _____

10. newton herald and messenger (newspaper) _____

B *Write each sentence correctly. Capitalize each title. Then underline or add quotation marks to set off the title.*

1. My life as a fifth-grade comedian is a very funny book!

_____

2. I enjoyed reading Anansi and the globe of light in this book of short stories.

_____

3. The little light in the back of my mind is the title of a poem I wrote.

_____

4. Monica sang I've been working on the railroad in the talent show.

_____

5. You'll find the book graveyard of the dinosaurs in the nonfiction section.

_____

6. Did you read the headlines in today's issue of the newport journal and sun?

_____

7. The eagle, the raven, and the whale is the title of Chapter 9.

_____

C   Sara wrote an article at the end of the school year about the reading assignments that the fifth graders most enjoyed. In her article, she made six mistakes when writing titles. Use the proofreading marks in the box to correct the errors.

 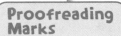
This year's fifth graders read many books, poems, and short stories. The students nominated their favorites and made a list of them.

There were many nominees for short stories. The short story "Song of The Trees" was Jessica's favorite. There were many nominees for books, too. Jamil recalled reading The Secret Garden and loving it. He thought the chapter called "the Key to the Garden" was particularly exciting. Several students thought <u>Keeper of the doves</u> was the best book they'd ever read. The funny Shel Silverstein poem It's All the Same to the Clam" made it to the list, too. In fact, several of Silverstein's poems made the list. For Pam, "Where the Sidewalk Ends was a favorite. The idea in this poem had great meaning for her.

Many other titles were nominated, and students were enthusiastic about all of them. In the end, everyone agreed that each one of the nominated titles was a winner.

Proofreading Marks

∧	Add
⊙	Period
ℯ	Take out
≡	Capital letter
/	Small letter

Did you correct the six mistakes in the titles?

WRITE

D *Read the description of each make-believe item. Then make up a title for it. Write your title on the line.*

1. a poem about a father who tries unsuccessfully to bake a cake

_____

2. a song about ice skating

_____

3. a magazine for kids who like computers

_____

4. a book about some fifth graders who travel to the future in a time machine

_____

5. a poem about a noisy blue jay

_____

6. a newspaper for people who live in the town of Green Valley

_____

7. a song about a big family reunion

_____

8. a magazine article about bicycle safety for young riders

_____

9. a chapter from a book about a family traveling west in a covered wagon

_____

Proofreading Checklist ☑

❏ *Did you begin the first word in each title with a capital letter?*
❏ *Did you begin every important word with a capital letter?*
❏ *Did you set off each title correctly?*

Lesson 48: Commas in a Series

LEARN

A **comma** separates words or ideas in a sentence and tells the reader when to pause.

Use commas to separate items in a series. A **series** is a list of three or more words or phrases. A conjunction such as *and* or *or* is used before the last item. Do not use a comma after the last item.

Words in a Series
We're going to a lake on **Friday, Saturday, and Sunday.**

Our cabin near the lake is **small, comfortable, and inexpensive**.

I might **fish, snorkel, swim, or sail** over the weekend.

Phrases in a Series
Our family **packs the van, climbs in, and drives north**.

PRACTICE

A *In each sentence, the words or phrases in a series are in **boldface**. Add commas to separate the words or phrases.*

1. We have left the **suburbs malls and highways** behind.

2. Everyone **talks laughs and relaxes**.

3. We **tell jokes listen to CDs and sing songs**.

4. **Villages farms forests and lakes** sweep past us.

5. **A hawk an owl or an eagle** flies high over the country road.

6. The sun **turns dark red sinks lower and finally disappears**.

7. We reach a **narrow steep and bumpy** driveway.

8. Dad **finds the key unlocks the cabin door and pushes it open**.

9. I drag in my **suitcase pillow and fishing tackle**.

10. We eat hamburgers with **ketchup lettuce and pickles** for supper.

B *Underline the series of words or phrases in each sentence. Add commas to separate the words or phrases.*

1. The weather is bright sunny and warm when I wake up.

2. The lake water ripples flashes and waves in the sunlight.

3. My father brother sister and I rush to the dock.

4. A canoe a rowboat and a sailboat bob up and down there.

5. We want to go boating fishing or swimming in the afternoon.

6. I trip over a loose board lose my balance and tumble into the lake!

7. The water is warm shallow and clear.

8. Dad shakes his head bends down and pulls me out.

9. I change my clothes eat breakfast and head for the rowboat.

10. We carry towels life preservers and fishing rods.

11. The old oars splash into the water creak loudly and move the boat.

12. We row to a spot in the lake that is quiet shady and rocky.

13. We cast out our lines wait a while and then reel the fish in.

14. We try real worms rubber worms and pumpernickel bread for bait.

15. We catch three small trout two perch and a ten-pound catfish!

C *The family found this list of rules at the cabin they rented. They noticed eight places where commas are missing from a series. They also noticed two places with unnecessary commas. Use the proofreading marks in the box to correct the mistakes.*

 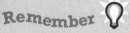
Proofreading Marks

∧	Add
⊙	Period
ℒ	Take out
≡	Capital letter
/	Small letter

Cabin Rules

✳ Please place all glass plastic and metal containers in the appropriate trash cans. Garbage pickup is on Mondays Wednesdays, and Saturdays.

✳ Do not leave garbage in the outside garbage cans overnight! Raccoons, bears, and other wild animals will find it!

✳ The dock and float are for your enjoyment. Feel free to wade swim, or sunbathe. Read the pamphlet on water safety before using the boats. Life preservers oars and canoe paddles are in the shed.

✳ Please keep the volume low on all TVs, radios, and electronic devices. Everyone is here to enjoy the peace, and quiet.

✳ Call Don Kane at 555-4354 if you experience any problems with the furnace, appliances plumbing, or electricity.

✳ Please shut all windows lock both doors, and mail the key to Don when it's time to leave. Remember to remove all food from the refrigerator, and cupboards.

Did you correct eight places where commas were omitted from a series? Did you take out two unnecessary commas?

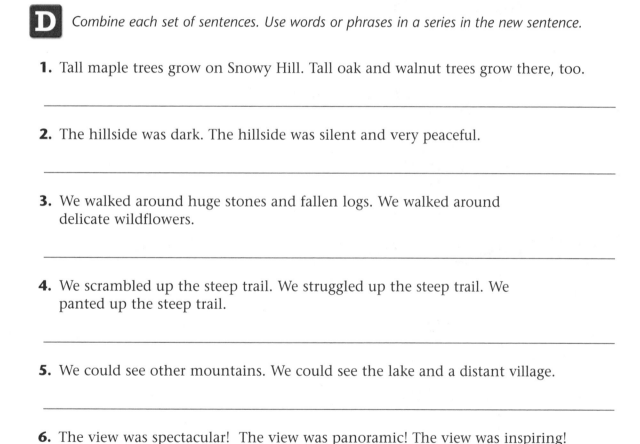

Online   For grammar games and activities, visit
www.grammarworkshop.com.

WRITE

To make your writing sound smoother, you can use words or phrases in a series to combine two or three sentences.

SEPARATE	This morning, we packed our binoculars. We climbed up Snowy Hill and looked for birds.
COMBINED	This morning, we packed our binoculars, climbed up Snowy Hill, and looked for birds.
SEPARATE	I saw a catbird. I saw a bluebird. I saw a cardinal, too.
COMBINED	I saw a catbird, a bluebird, and a cardinal.

D *Combine each set of sentences. Use words or phrases in a series in the new sentence.*

1. Tall maple trees grow on Snowy Hill. Tall oak and walnut trees grow there, too.

_____

2. The hillside was dark. The hillside was silent and very peaceful.

_____

3. We walked around huge stones and fallen logs. We walked around delicate wildflowers.

_____

4. We scrambled up the steep trail. We struggled up the steep trail. We panted up the steep trail.

_____

5. We could see other mountains. We could see the lake and a distant village.

_____

6. The view was spectacular! The view was panoramic! The view was inspiring!

_____

**Go back to the sentences you wrote.
Underline the series in each sentence.**

Lesson 49: **More Commas**

LEARN

■ Here are some more uses for commas.

- Use a comma to set off introductory words such as *yes*, *no*, or *well*.
  Yes, we celebrate Earth Day on April 22.
  No, it isn't a national holiday.
  Well, people celebrate Earth Day in many ways.

- Use a comma after an introductory word that shows mild feeling. A word that shows feeling or emotion is an **interjection**. *Hey, oh, hooray, wow,* and *ah* are interjections.
  Wow, what a great idea for a holiday!

- Use a comma to set off the name of a person being spoken to or addressed. The comma might come before, after, or both before and after a **noun of direct address**.
  Today is Earth Day, **Juan**!
  Juan, today is Earth Day!
  Did you know, **Juan**, that today is Earth Day?

- Use a comma after an introductory prepositional phrase.
  Across the world, people celebrate Earth Day.

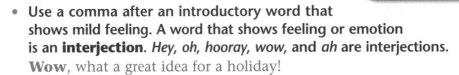

PRACTICE

A *Read each sentence. Write **introductory word, interjection, noun of direct address,** or **introductory prepositional phrase** to tell what words are set off by the comma or commas.*

1. Mrs. Davis, many people are worried about the planet Earth. _____

2. Yes, many serious problems face our planet. _____

3. Oh, so many animals and plants are struggling to survive! _____

4. In some countries, people don't have enough clean water. _____

5. Clean air, Raoul, is in short supply in some places.

_____

6. We address these issues on Earth Day, Gerri.

_____

7. No, we can't solve serious problems in a single day.

_____

8. Hey, it is important to start working on them!

_____

9. Well, there are many things we can do.

_____

10. After all, we have only one planet to live on.

_____

B *Read each sentence. Add commas where they are needed.*

1. Our fifth grade has planned many activities for Earth Day Mr. Samuels.

2. For one thing we're planting three trees in the playground.

3. Yes the trees were donated by Nelson's Nursery again this year.

4. Wow they have done so much to help our school!

5. The park cleanup Elisa is scheduled for next week.

6. No we still don't have enough volunteers.

7. By April 19 all jobs will be assigned.

8. How many posters Jason have you made for Walk to School Day?

9. Yes I agree that we will need at least eight posters.

10. Oh that poster design is really creative!

11. In my opinion reminding people to recycle is very important.

12. With all our planning this will be the best Earth Day ever!

C *Edie wrote a short speech to give at the Earth Day assembly. In these paragraphs from her speech, she forgot to write eight commas. Find the mistakes, and use the proofreading marks in in the box to correct them.*

The United States celebrated the first Earth Day on April 22, 1970. More than 20 million Americans took part. Wow what an incredible turnout that was! Nearly every city and school in the nation had special activities.

On that first Earth Day members of the U.S. Congress did not meet. No they went to classes instead to learn how to care for the earth. Ordinary citizens also took time off. Yes millions of Americans that day went on nature walks, studied pollution, and learned about recycling.

Classmates, that first Earth Day was a great success! People formed car pools to conserve fuel. Recycling and litter campaigns got started. In the nation's capital Congress set up the Environmental Protection Agency. Well that government agency has helped clean our air, water, and land.

Friends we need to remember the excitement of that first Earth Day. Yes we Americans have grown careless. We have begun to waste our water, fuel, forests, and land again. We must get busy. We must do all that we can do to repair our damaged planet Earth.

Proofreading Marks

∧	Add
⊙	Period
ℒ	Take out
≡	Capital letter
/	Small letter

Did you add a comma in eight places?

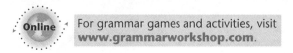

WRITE

D *Imagine that you are part of the Earth Day cleanup committee. Write a sentence that responds to each statement below. Use the type of word or phrase in parentheses in each sentence. Make up any information that you need. The first one is done for you.*

1. Sarah asks when the park cleanup begins. (noun of direct address)

  Sarah, the park cleanup begins at 4 o'clock on April 22.

2. Inez says more than 100 students have signed up for the park cleanup. (interjection)

3. Ari asks when the class will celebrate Earth Day. (introductory prepositional phrase)

4. Sheila wants to know what the Eyes on Recycling program is. (noun of direct address)

5. Tomas asks if school is closed on Earth Day. (introductory word)

6. Jill says that all the fifth graders are walking to school on Earth Day. (interjection)

7. Evan wants to know what he can do for Earth Day. (noun of direct address)

8. Mrs. Guerino asks whether Earth Day was a success. (introductory word)

Proofreading Checklist ✔

❑ *Did you use the type of word or phrase specified in parentheses?*

❑ *Did you use commas to set off introductory words, interjections, nouns of direct address, and introductory prepositional phrases?*

Lesson 50: **Parts of a Letter**

LEARN

■ A **friendly letter** is an informal letter to someone you know well. In a friendly letter, the **greeting** and **closing** begin with a capital letter and end with a comma. In the **heading**, a comma separates the city and state and also the day and the year.

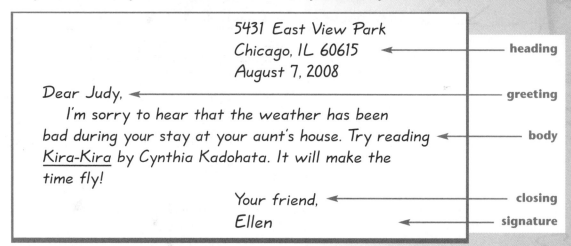

5431 East View Park
Chicago, IL 60615 ← **heading**
August 7, 2008

Dear Judy, ← **greeting**
    I'm sorry to hear that the weather has been bad during your stay at your aunt's house. Try reading ← **body** Kira-Kira by Cynthia Kadohata. It will make the time fly!

               Your friend, ← **closing**
               Ellen ← **signature**

■ A **business letter** is a formal letter to someone you do not know well. It has an **inside address**, which gives the name and address of the organization or person you are writing to. Place the **title** of the person after the person's name. Use a **colon (:)** at the end of the greeting, and end with a formal closing.

496 Gold Avenue
Dublin, OH 43016 ← **heading**
August 10, 2008

Ms. Jenna Johnson, Director
Fairfax Public Library
812 Maple Avenue ← **inside address**
Dublin, OH 43016

Dear Ms. Johnson: ← **greeting**

    Would the Fairfax Public Library be able to order a copy of Kira-Kira by Cynthia Kadohata? ← **body**

           Yours truly, ← **closing**
           Judy Richards ← **signature**
           Judy Richards

PRACTICE

A *Rewrite each letter part. Use correct capitalization and punctuation.*

1. June 4 2009 _____

2. dear Senator _____

3. respectfully _____

4. your cousin _____

B *Complete each letter with the missing letter part. Write the letter part correctly.*

| your pal | 496 Gold avenue | dear Ellen | Dublin OH 43016 |

_____

_____

September 1, 2008

_____

    Thanks for the tip about <u>Kira-Kira</u>. It was really great! I have an idea. Why don't we start a book club in school this fall? We could read and discuss books. Let me know if you would like to help me start the club.

_____

Judy

C *Ellen wrote this letter. She made three mistakes in the use of punctuation and two mistakes in the use of capital letters. Read the letter, and find the mistakes. Use the proofreading marks in the box to correct them.*

Remember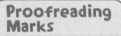
Use a comma after the greeting in a friendly letter. Use a colon after the greeting in a business letter.

Proofreading Marks

∧	Add
⊙	Period
ℰ	Take out
≡	Capital letter
/	Small letter

5431 East View Park

Chicago, IL 60615

December 15 2008

Ms. Dana Obermeyer, School Librarian

Kane Elementary School

2426 Elm Street

Chicago, IL 60615

dear Ms. Obermeyer,

　　The Book Club's recent used-book sale was a great success! In all, we raised $247.50 selling used and donated books. The other club members and I have decided to donate this money to the school library. We hope you can use it to buy new fiction and nonfiction books.

　　　　　　　　　　sincerely yours:

　　　　　　　　　　Ellen Phillips

　　　　　　　　　　Ellen Phillips

Did you correct three mistakes with punctuation and two mistakes with capital letters?

WRITE

Online For grammar games and activities, visit
www.grammarworkshop.com.

D *Write a friendly letter or a business letter. If you write a friendly
letter, tell a friend about a club that you would like to start in
your school. If you write a business letter, ask a teacher or principal in
your school for information about how to start your club.*

Proofreading Checklist ✔

❏ *Did you use commas and capital letters correctly in your letter?*

❏ *Did you use a comma after the greeting if you wrote a friendly
letter?*

❏ *Did you use a colon after the greeting if you wrote a
business letter?*

Lesson 51: **Quotations**

LEARN

■ A **direct quotation** is a speaker's exact words. Enclose a direct quotation in quotation marks, and capitalize the first word.

> Mom said, "**M**onday is Dad's birthday."

- Use a comma to separate a direct quotation from the rest of the sentence. If the quotation comes at the end of the sentence, place the comma *before* the quotation. If the quotation comes at the beginning, place the comma *inside* the end quotation mark.
> Joe said**,** "Let's buy Dad a gift."
> "Let's buy Dad a gift**,**" Joe said.

- If the quotation is a question or an exclamation, do not use a comma. Instead, place the question mark or exclamation mark *inside* the quotation marks.
> "Dad would love a DVD player**!**" exclaimed Gina.

- If a quotation is divided, put each part in quotation marks. If the second part of the divided quotation continues the first part, begin it with a small letter.
> "A DVD player," said Mom, "**w**ould be the perfect gift."

■ An **indirect quotation** does not give the speaker's exact words. Do *not* use quotation marks for an indirect quotation.

> **DIRECT** Mom said, "Try to shop wisely."
> **INDIRECT** Mom said we should try to shop wisely.

PRACTICE

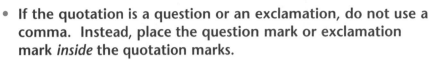

A *Read each sentence. If it contains a direct quotation, underline all the exact words in the quotation. If it contains an indirect quotation, circle the sentence.*

1. "Before we buy," Mom said, "we should do some comparison shopping."

2. "What is comparison shopping?" asked Gina.

3. "When you comparison shop," explained Mom, "you compare the price of the same item at different stores."

4. "Look at the difference in price in these two stores," said Gina.

5. Joe said that the DVD player costs $10 more at Marty's Best than at Electronics and Beyond.

6. "It's cheaper at Electronics and Beyond," said Joe, "so let's buy it there."

7. "But Marty's Best doesn't charge tax," Mom said, "and it's right here in town."

8. Gina said that comparison shopping gave them a lot of information.

9. Joe said, "I see that price isn't the only thing to consider."

10. Gina agreed, "We have to consider convenience, too."

B *Rewrite each sentence that contains a direct quotation. Use quotation marks, capital letters, and punctuation marks correctly to show a speaker's exact words. Circle the sentence if it contains an indirect quotation.*

1. What is a good way to save money asked Rosa. _____

_____

2. Alan exclaimed I know a great way to save. _____

_____

3. One way is to set limits he said. _____

_____

4. Terry asked why limits are important. _____

_____

5. Setting limits Alan answered tells you how much you can spend. _____

_____

C *Rosa wrote this story about how she began saving money. When writing direct quotations in her story, she omitted six quotation marks, one comma, and one end punctuation mark. Use the proofreading marks in the box to correct her mistakes.*

Proofreading Marks

∧	Add
⊙	Period
℘	Take out
≡	Capital letter
/	Small letter

When I was five, my grandmother gave me a plastic pig with a slot on its back. "What's this for? I asked.

"It's a piggy bank, Grandma laughed. She told me to put any leftover change into the pig.

Why should I do that?" I asked.

"Coins grow into dollars," she said.

After that, instead of spending my change on snacks and toys, I dropped my coins into the pig.

"Has that pig put on any weight" Grandma asked me when she visited three months later.

"It sure has! I exclaimed. Together, we shook all the coins out of the pig.

"There's $21.44 here" Grandma counted. She took $21 worth of coins and gave me a $20 bill and a $1 bill to put back in the pig. "Keep putting your coins in," she said, and we'll count them again the next time I visit."

When I was ten, I had more than $450 in that pig. It's definitely time for you to open up a savings account at the bank," Grandma announced. So that's what I did.

LOOK Back **Did you find six missing quotation marks, one missing comma, and one missing end punctuation mark?**

Online For grammar games and activities, visit
www.grammarworkshop.com.

WRITE

D *A group of students in Rosa's class is having a
discussion about saving money. Read the beginning
of the conversation. Then continue the conversation on the
lines below. Share your own ideas about saving money.*

"Why should we save our money?" asked Brad.
"Why not just spend everything and have a good
time now?"

"You need to save," replied Alan, "if you ever
want to have enough money to buy something
that costs a little more."

"It's hard to save," said Rosa. "It means not
getting things you want today."

"Still, I think saving is important," Ray added.

_____

_____

_____

_____

_____

_____

_____

_____

_____

Proofreading Checklist ☑

❑ *Did you put quotation marks before and after each
speaker's exact words?*

❑ *Did you capitalize the first word of each quotation?*

❑ *Did you punctuate each direct quotation correctly?*

Writing Sentences Correctly (pp. 200–203) *Write these sentences correctly. Use capital letters and the correct end punctuation marks.*

1. we will go skiing in January can you join us _____

_____

2. what a short month February is _____

_____

3. turn your clocks ahead one hour _____

_____

4. why are there so many April showers _____

_____

Capitalizing Proper Nouns and Adjectives (pp. 204–207)
Read each sentence. Write each proper noun or proper adjective correctly.

5. We visited redwood state park. _____

6. Have you ever been to a mexican city? _____

7. Show me the persian gulf on the map. _____

8. When is earth day this year? _____

Abbreviations (pp. 208–211) *Write each item correctly.*

9. dr Mary r Meyers _____

10. fri, Dec. 9 _____

11. Royal Baking co _____

12. po. box 40 _____

Titles (pp. 212–215) *Write each title correctly.*

13. We read the novel julie of the wolves.   _____

14. She sang red sails in the sunset in the talent show.   _____

15. Living with Volcanoes is an interesting article.   _____

16. The pit and the pendulum is Poe's best short story.   _____

Commas (pp. 216–223) *In each sentence, add commas where they are needed.*

17. My father sister and I painted the house garage and fence.

18. We mixed paint painted walls and cleaned brushes until August.

19. Jason is September your favorite month of the year?

20. Yes it just might be my favorite month Marie.

21. For one thing I like the cool weather in autumn.

22. Wow this cool autumn breeze feels great!

Parts of a Letter (pp. 224–227) *Write each letter part correctly.*

23. sincerely   _____

24. greenville, SC   _____

25. June 23 2009   _____

26. Dear sir   _____

Quotations (pp. 228–231) *Add commas and quotation marks where they are needed. Circle the sentence if it is an indirect quotation.*

27. Is Thanksgiving always on a Thursday? Kelly asked.

28. Matt explained that it's the third Thursday in November.

29. When I hear the word *December* said Kelly I think about the holidays.

30. Janet exclaimed The holidays are a great way to end the year!

DIRECTIONS *Fill in the circle next to the sentence that shows the correct use of commas, capital letters, end marks, and quotation marks.*

1. ○ We may move to Green View Apartments.

○ "Deidre, Mom told me, we've been on a list for this apartment."

○ We can move in on july 31 or august 1.

○ Mom and I drove down rte. 136 to see it.

2. ○ Yes, the apartments are really nice.

○ They are sunny safe and modern.

○ "You'll like living next to green view park," Mom said.

○ I shrugged and sighed, nodded, and agreed.

3. ○ Why don't I feel excited about moving.

○ Maya, Jen, and Lee, all live on Jay street.

○ Am I ever lucky to have them as Friends.

○ "We're friends forever," we tell each other.

4. ○ We all play for the Jay Street eagles.

○ Jen asked, "Who will pitch for our team?"

○ We're all in the School Band, too.

○ "When The Saints Go Marching in" is our theme song.

5. ○ Yes I know Jay Street has some problems.

○ It has litter old houses and heavy traffic.

○ It is the only home that I have ever had.

○ Do you understand how I feel.

6. ○ On tuesday I went to the new library.

○ Mr. Li checked out my book Stepping On The Cracks.

○ "Are you moving Deidre"? Mr. Li asked.

○ "Yes, I'm afraid so," I said.

7. ○ Jen and I biked to east lake yesterday.

○ We've spent so many Summer days there.

○ "Will you still swim here," Jen asked, "after you move away?"

○ "Well I don't know" I replied.

8. ○ We passed the arts center, and our library.

○ Wow, I'll really miss them, too?

○ We walked down Cedar Street.

○ Why did we have to move anyway.

DIRECTIONS *Read the letter, and look carefully at each underlined part. Fill in the circle next to the answer choice that shows the correct use of commas, capital letters, end marks, and quotation marks. If the underlined part is already correct, fill in the circle for "Correct as is."*

204 Jay Street
Madison, WI 53704
August 1, 2008

<u>mr. Aaron Smith, Director</u>
        (9)
Green View Apartments
2459 Davenport Road
Cottage Grove, WI 53527

<u>dear mr Smith</u>,
   (10)

    After careful consideration, my daughter and I have decided not to move

into the apartment in Building 13C of your housing complex. Yes, the

apartment is <u>sunny spacious and appealing</u>. At the moment, however, our
                 (11)
present apartment and neighborhood seem to suit us better.

    Thank you for your help.

                <u>yours truly</u>
                  (12)
                Sara Jamison
                Sara Jamison

9. ○ mr Aaron Smith, Director
   ○ Mr Aaron Smith, Director
   ○ Mr. Aaron Smith, Director
   ○ Correct as is

10. ○ dear Mr Smith,
    ○ Dear Mr. Smith:
    ○ Dear Mr. Smith,
    ○ Correct as is

11. ○ sunny, spacious, and appealing
    ○ sunny, spacious and appealing
    ○ sunny spacious, and appealing
    ○ Correct as is

12. ○ Yours truly:
    ○ Yours truly,
    ○ Yours Truly,
    ○ Correct as is

INDEX

HOW TO USE PROOFREADING MARKS

The following paragraph illustrates all of the proofreading marks shown in the chart.

My family hiked the appalachian Trail last year. The trail runs for 2174 miles from Georgia to Maine. We started at the beginning of the Trail and hiked up to Springer Mountain. We climbed up rocky ground and stone steps. When we got to the top, we could see for miles. What a great day we had!

Proofreading Marks

∧	Add
⊙	Period
℘	Take out
≡	Capital letter
/	Small letter